Edmund Burke and the Discourse of Virtue

STUDIES IN RHETORIC AND COMMUNICATION
General Editors:
E. Culpepper Clark
Raymie E. McKerrow
David Zarefsky

Stephen H. Browne

Edmund Burke and the Discourse of Virtue

The University of Alabama Press   Tuscaloosa and London

Copyright © 1993
The University of Alabama Press
Tuscaloosa, Alabama 35487–0380
All rights reserved
Manufactured in the United States of America

∞

The paper on which this book is printed meets the minimum
requirements of American National Standard for Information
Science-Permanence of Paper for Printed Library Materials,
ANSI Z39.48-1984.

Library of Congress Cataloging-in-Publication Data

Browne, Stephen H.
    Edmund Burke and the discourse of virtue / Stephen H. Browne.
        p.   cm.—(Studies in rhetoric and communication)
    Includes bibliographical references and index.
    ISBN 0-8173-0676-5 (alk. paper)
    1. Burke, Edmund, 1729–1797—Criticism and interpretation.   2. Great
Britain—Politics and government—18th century—Historiography.   3. Speeches,
addresses, etc., English—History and criticism.   4. Political oratory—Great
Britain—History—18th century.   5. Ethics—Great Britain—History—18th
century.   6. Rhetoric—1500–1800.   7. Virtue.   I. Title.   II. Series.
PR3334.B4Z57   1993
824'.6—dc20   92-46656

British Library Cataloguing-in-Publication Data available

This Book is
Dedicated to
Margaret,
Lovingly.

Contents

Acknowledgments

Chapter 1 originally appeared as "Edmund Burke's *Discontents* and the Interpretation of Political Culture," *Quarterly Journal of Speech* 77 (1991): 53–66, copyright 1991 by the Speech Communication Association; used by permission. Chapter 3 originally appeared as "Burke's *Speech on Conciliation:* The Pragmatic Basis of Rhetorical Judgment," in *Texts in Context: Critical Dialogues on Significant Episodes in American Political Rhetoric*, ed. Michael C. Leff and Fred J. Kauffeld, 55–80 (Davis, Calif.: Hermagoras Press, 1989), copyright 1989 by Michael C. Leff and Fred J. Kauffeld; used by permission. Chapter 6 originally appeared as "Edmund Burke's Letter to a Noble Lord: A Textual Study in Political Philosophy and Rhetorical Action," *Communication Monographs* 55 (1988): 215–29, copyright 1988 by the Speech Communication Association; used by permission.

The following have contributed, each in their own way and some perhaps unknowingly, to the inception, development, and completion of this book: James R. Andrews, Thomas W. Benson, Edwin Black, Lloyd F. Bitzer, David E. Browne, John A. Campbell, James M. Farrell, Dilip Parameshwar Gaonkar, Dennis S. Gouran, G. Jack Gravlee, Robert S. Iltis, James R. Irvine, Fred J. Kauffeld, John Lucaites, Stephen E. Lucas, Thomas Rosteck, and Howard Weinbrot. To each I am grateful. My greatest debt is of course to Michael C. Leff, my friend and teacher still.

Edmund Burke and the Discourse of Virtue

Introduction
Reading Edmund Burke

Those of you who have visited England's National Portrait Gallery know of its splendid collection of works by Sir Joshua Reynolds. In the summer of 1985 I had made my way to the gallery in hopes of seeing Reynolds' portrait of Edmund Burke. I expected to see it hanging there, somewhere between the oddly comical aspect of Goldsmith and the dour visage of Dr. Johnson. I found, to my great disappointment, that Burke's portrait had been recently removed to one of those mysterious rooms where paintings are stored, cleaned, relegated. It seemed to me then, and does so now, that something similar has happened to the historical Burke. This historical Burke, of course, is also a representation, or rather a series of them. Thus I have in mind no grand search for the "real" Burke, if only because modern thought so relentlessly warns against such fictions. I am more concerned that Burke has in some sense been taken away, that we have lost sight of a figure at once commanding, elusive, and complex. Whether he is, in his absence, being cleaned up or stored away until we have more space to accommodate him, I could not say. This book, in any event, represents my attempt to recall Burke from storage and present him again as a subject of public attention.

This said, it must be readily admitted that Burke has not suffered from any lack of scholarly interest in the last half-century. If anything, he seems to have yielded himself too easily, ready in any given surge of revisionism to offer the poignant maxim, the lesson on political wisdom or folly. Burke may in this sense be said to have many reputations; as a result, any one interpretation seems inevitably to contest every other. All this is as it should be, this "Burke for all seasons," and I have no interest here in silencing any of these alternative voices. They are in any case too diverse, and some too interesting in their own right, to dismiss as falling short of the mark. Catharine Macaulay and Thomas Paine, Coleridge and Shelley, Sir Leslie Stephen and Sir Lewis Namier: these and many others have alternately championed and reviled Burke, and there is no evidence to suggest that he will cease provoking useful work.[1]

What can it mean, then, to suggest that Burke has been somehow spirited away? Only this: in the relentless process of appropriation and reappropriation, we have managed too often to reduce Burke to a set of propositions. The result is to lose sight of Burke as an artist, a fully embodied, three-dimensional master of rhetoric and oratory. We have, in that stead, statements about his statements. These declaratives have come to represent what Burke is all about: what he said about a given issue, what his ideas imply about this or that theory of human nature or politics. We are presented, consequently, with a group of adjectives that structure our ways of reading Burke: reactionary; romantic; utilitarian; liberal; conservative; inevitably, neo-versions of these all.[2]

Whatever the merits of or motives for any particular label, however appealing the ideological claim, this reduction of Burke's writing to propositional utility is, in effect, to remove him from his place on the wall. But put him back up there, among friends and enemies, and another Burke can be seen, a more fully human and flawed, certainly a more interesting Burke: a public figure—stylized, complex, inconsistent, and habitual—a man who cannot be understood independent of his modes of presentation. So completely, so deeply did Burke live the political life that he could only understand himself within and through its language. That is why the propositional Burke will never do: it must fail to account for the rhetorical Burke, the Burke who could not apprehend any distinction between the idea and the word, the principle and its expression. Such a Burke, by extension, requires and rewards a different kind of reading, an approach sensitive to his language without aestheticizing it, and comprehending his ideas without reifying them. This new way of interpreting Burke reflects broadly the aims of this study.[3]

But perhaps I have leaned on the trope too heavily; my hope is not to put Burke back where he "belongs." I have no more proprietary rights to his legacy that anyone else, and I am skeptical of those who would fix him in any one place. The goal, rather, is to hold him up where we can take a better look. Here we are able to confront Burke's rhetorical artistry head-on and to see in his writings, not princi-

ples struggling to escape the confines of language, but language—
ingenious, cunning, self-promoting and other-regarding, seductive
and abusive—giving life and power to principle. In coming to understand this discourse, we discover an unabashedly rhetorical character,
a personality fully realized and disclosed only as he engaged and was
engaged by public controversy. Far from wishing away Burke's rhetorical habits, therefore, these essays take them as its very subject
matter. Reading Burke as a rhetorical artist means making no apologies for his partisan motives, his appeals to emotion as prompts to
reasonable action, and his use of aesthetic convention for practical
purposes. These are the very stuff of Burke's art.

If there is a unity to Burke's discourse, it is not to be found at the
level of systematic theory. It is, rather, to be discovered in recurrent
forms of thematic expression, where generalized principles get invoked and configured for specific purposes. Here then is our point of
entry: the stated assumption that Burke's art is an artistry of ideas
shaped, driven, and warranted by the demands of public action. This
perspective on Burke—as first and most importantly a rhetorical
artist—commits us from the outset to a problem within criticism.
At a general level it leads us to ask how to reconcile technical craft
and substantive principle in accounting for rhetorical excellence.
Our answer must be qualified by two considerations. First, this book
is not about the greater points of conflict between philosophy and
rhetoric, which have traditionally posed this question; it cannot
therefore articulate this enduring tension in systematic fashion. Second, the tradition that informs and sets the terms for that debate is
still very much under construction. But to the extent that it bears,
directly or otherwise, on my interpretation of Burke's rhetorical art,
it deserves preliminary recognition.

To put the matter simply: what can be meant when I announce
that Burke was eloquent and ought therefore to be read as a significant and serious thinker? Does this claim, hardly provocative on its
face, mean that Burke is a master craftsman, one who commands
the technical possibilities embedded in the language? A stylist, in
short, interesting because his prose is in some sense compelling as
an artistic production? One can certainly pursue an argument along
these lines; critics have, in fact, been doing so on and off for two
hundred years. A few short generations ago, Burke was held to be an
exemplar of English prose, his *Speech on Conciliation* forced upon
unwitting schoolchildren as a model for "doing it right."

The basis for judging Burke's art in this way is essentially aesthetic, and therein lies half the problem. Consider the following
passage from the oration just mentioned: "For some time past the
Old World has been fed from the New. The scarcity which you had

felt would have been a desolating famine, if this child of your old age, with a true filial piety, with a Roman charity, had not put the full breast of its youthful exuberance to the mouth of its exhausted parent." How are we to make sense of this language? One conventional approach is to translate it into literature and, by applying somewhat crude standards, hold it forth as an isolated example of aesthetic ingenuity. Among its other limitations, this emphasis on aesthetic prowess ignores the entirety of the given discourse and misses the more general patterns of meaning and the unfolding action of the text. In Burke's case, he was capable within a single oration of reaching the heights of eloquence and the depths of wretched puns, tedium, and impropriety. Aesthetisizing Burke, more importantly, misses the point; it requires that he be snatched away from his familiar ground, his public space, and be evaluated according to standards alien to his eminently practical craft. This is not to say that Burke's rhetoric does not evince an aesthetic sensibility. In fact he had a deeply figurative mind, and he routinely presented his ideas in language that put images, tropes, and linguistic novelty in the foreground. But to recognize this and integrate it into a general account of Burke's rhetorical craft is patently different than rendering his art into formalist and technical terms. To read Burke rhetorically is to recall at every step that he was an orator—a public man who, even in his letters and essays, was at once engaged and constrained by the expectations of the public mind.

Although Burke has been the object of critics who would transform him into a polite essayist, he has served just as often the purposes of political theorists. Here we have a counterpart to the first tradition I have identified: concerned not at all with Burke's rhetorical craft, they have discovered in his writings a deep and many-layered bedrock of ideas. We have touched on this facet of Burke's legacy briefly and noted how it encourages a process of reduction to proposition. However careful, however convincing this approach to Burke as an ideological spokesman, the outcome is almost inevitably plagued by complexities and contradictions. We have only, for instance, to note the hopelessness of fixing Burke as the founder of modern conservatism—this advocate for Irish liberties, this leader of economic reform, this supporter of colonial aspirations, this relentless enemy of crimes against East India, this proponent of Catholic relief. Superimposing categories generated out of cold war ambitions onto an eighteenth-century British statesman is in any case a project doomed to failure of an abject kind.

There is, however, a way out of this dilemma, false as it is, this pull toward aesthetic technique on the one hand and systematic abstraction on the other. One approach is to locate within the technical lore of the art an unexpectedly rich, even architechtonic principle. What, for example, had been routinely regarded as merely formulary can be reinvested with great explanatory power; rules or techniques get emancipated and fully realized as constitutive elements of the rhetorical art. We have, in the last two decades, seen a remarkable explosion in just this kind of interpretive activity. Much of its animus comes from continental predispositions; its success can be measured by the fact that no figure of style can be thought safe from being transformed, for the moment at least, into an Ur-trope of passing but spectacular importance. American rhetorical critics have pursued recognizably similar paths—if for different reasons and with different results.

This book opts for a second approach. I conduct this study of Burke's rhetorical artistry as I do not out of complaint with the above perspective, but because the texts themselves invite a different tact. My reading might be thought of as the converse of finding general principles within technical craft. I am concerned to locate the craft in the principle. Put another way, the following essays are designed to explain how certain normative principles get managed within the constraints and possibilities of their public presentation. I take this management to be rhetorical in motive, if not always in effect. I am anxious, moreover, to emphasize a premise directing my interpretation of Burke's art: that principles as such, and virtue in particular, have for Burke no status or stature independent of their rhetorical expression. I am concerned, in short, to understand how a principle like virtue is made meaningful in and through the public vocabulary of shared interests, motives, and aspirations.

Does this aim require a "theory" of virtue? If we take theory at minimum to signify a relatively stable and internally consistent set of explanatory propositions; if it describes a limited number of precepts able to account for an indefinite variety of phenomena, then I do not believe that Burke can be said to have offered a theory of virtue. Nor can it be proven that Burke conceived of some concept like virtue to function as an ultimate ground, unchanging and monolithic, for his arguments. That he invoked the word and its attending commonplaces regularly is apparent to any careful reader, and that he deployed it routinely as a legitimizing principle is equally clear. But recurrent use and strategic reference do not take us very far. We are left with the question of what virtue can do to help us better apprehend Burke's distinctive artistry. There are, after all, a good many concepts that may be plausibly offered in its place as having greater interpretive force. Why virtue?

Virtue was for Burke a pervasive subject, warrant, and reward for rhetorical action. As sweeping as this claim is, it can nevertheless be substantiated, and the following essays are designed to serve this function. He did not, to my knowledge, ever bother to define virtue as such. But it is there in his early writings on political party; in his orations on American affairs; in his vindication of political judgment in his *Speech to the Electors of Bristol*; in his tireless campaign against Warren Hastings, a figure so contemptible to Burke as to represent a kind of antivirtue; and it is evident in his late writings, wherein virtue takes on personal and ideological significance and is finally blended into a vindication of self and country.

If pushed, we could probably find in Burke's writing an implicit theory of virtue—or at least a set of relatively stable references. They would include classical as well as Christian allusions and would gather under a rather broad semantic arc such values as prudence, right reason, forbearance, magnanimity, order, reverence, fidelity, foresight, and steadfastness. Its ground he could locate in a very complex conception of human community; this conception, which occupies a good deal of the attention of the book itself, embraces human community as an expression of historical, religious, economic, and political achievement.

But even if the reader is willing to grant to virtue a significant presence in Burke's discourse, we still fall short of answering the question posed above: Why virtue? The answer is that, however diligently we try to coax from Burke a straightforward and strict definition of virtue, it can never be enough. Virtue was meaningful for Burke only as it was constituted in the active exchange between author and reader, speaker and audience. This is a rhetorical process and so provides the rationale for this study. Virtue is an achieved meaning, useful in political contexts as warrant for action; for Burke it is never a given, but rather a prerequisite for establishing the essential bonds of community out of which genuine discourse can occur.

Virtue is in this sense an active principle, best conceived as a dynamic commonplace, energized by the force of public controversy and validated by public will. As an inventive resource, it summons shared perceptions of the good to authorize action. As a distinctly rhetorical principle, it is renewed again and again in the face of situated needs and particular aims. Virtue is thus by necessity an unstable principle, at least partially so, because it is shaped and promoted by the volatile demands of human plurality. To understand virtue, then, is to see how it is made to configure public values. And to formulate virtue as a rhetorical principle is to see how it rationalizes the will to speak and how it serves as the means of social and symbolic inducement.

If this brief description sounds altogether too general, I can only hold out the hope that the textual readings will illustrate what is meant by a discourse of virtue. Clearly much has been omitted from my account. The reader will find no sustained attempt to confront or engage competing schools of Burkean studies; nor will the reader come across new insights into late eighteenth-century political or social life. Perhaps, in light of so much recent work on the idea of virtue itself, the reader will find most curious my refusal to engage Burke in current controversies. In part this is because I do not find philosophical disputes over the correct meaning of virtue to be particularly informative for understanding Burke's rhetorical art; in part it is because the work on virtue that is relevant to Burke's thought—especially that of J. G. A. Pocock—is so well established and so well articulated that I see no point in challenging it here. But most important for my purposes, I wish to offer interpretations, themselves no doubt strategic and stylized, that will reveal virtue-in-action, virtue, that is, as it is created in the distinctive space between source, subject, and audience. Here, it seems to me, is where Burke's principles are best understood, where this collaborative and tentative, this deeply human desire to move one another finds its medium.

Each of the following essays attempts to discover and dwell for a moment within these creative spaces. The objects of my analysis, the tracts, speeches, and public letters, I cannot present as representative of Burke's writing. There is no truly representative work in the first place, as students of Burke eventually come to realize, just as there is no typical example of any work of individual talent. The texts have been selected, rather, for the simple reason that they best illustrate my basic theme. Here we find six instances of Burke's discourse of virtue; each rotates our perspective on that theme in a different direction. Each, moreover, shows Burke at work confronting political realities, drawing upon his own resources and a collective legacy, and crafting a discourse aimed at remaking a world of which he was most surely a part. All of the texts are significant and well known to those familiar with Burke, the eighteenth century, or the history of public address. No two are alike, but they collectively present to the reader an extraordinary opportunity to see how a principle as complex and evasive as virtue gets promoted through rhetorical action.

Burke's *Thoughts on the Causes of the Present Discontents* (1770) represents his first major statement on the benefits of party. It has become in the years since something of a classic, and it continues to stimulate controversy over its origins, intentions, and influence. *Discontents* was preceded by two tracts containing the seeds of Burke's arguments on the nature of party, and it was followed by others reaffirming his commitment to party as a legitimate basis for political action. It is of interest here because it so well exemplifies Burke's skill in creating the most advantageous possible relationship between author and reader. *Discontents* generates and then nurtures what I have termed a process of "reading-with," wherein the reader comes to participate in Burke's argument because to do so itself constitutes an act of virtue. Promoting party as an expression of political unity and thus as a form of virtue, Burke induces the reader to collaborate in the rhetorical action of the text. The argument is thus a summons to virtue, ultimately realized in the consent of its implied reader.

Four years after the publication of *Discontents*, Burke delivered the first of two masterful orations on the colonial problem. *The Speech on Taxation* (1774), although not as widely hailed as the later *Speech on Conciliation with the Colonies* (1775), is in fact a virtuoso performance. Burke had already made his mark in Parliament as a speaker of unusual energy—if not restraint—and the address of 1774 confirmed his reputation as a first-class orator. Detailed, rigorous, unusually well informed, the speech stands as one of the most eloquent expressions of imperial obligation in the eighteenth century. It is, moreover, an exquisite statement on the relationship between political virtue and individual character. My reading of the speech stresses this relationship, perhaps to the exclusion of other important considerations. The focus is justified, indeed invited, by the series of character portraits that Burke presents. In strokes deft and sure, he sketches a virtual gallery of political personae, including the likes of Grenville, Townshend, North, and Chatham. The result is a study in virtue as it is embodied in human character, habits of mind made public by the demands of controversy and, of course, Burke's own artistry. It is this process of verbal portraiture that illuminates the rhetorical creation of virtue in the oration; as the reader/listener comes to witness these characters made public, we come to understand the psychological impulses toward virtue and its opposite. And the more elaborate, the more crafted and aesthetically compelling the portrait, the more convincing the argument.

To American readers Burke's *Speech on Conciliation* is perhaps most familiar. As a champion for colonial interests, Burke was tireless, and the speech embodies most fully his arguments for imperial tolerance. But it is notable as well for Burke's critique of political reason and for the ways in which he enacts an alternative model of deliberation. His attack on North's colonial policy, we shall see, is enlarged into an attack on abstract or speculative reasoning in political affairs. It is in some ways Burke's most extraordinary effort—

doomed to defeat in the short run, but claiming in the long run a place among the greatest deliberative exercises in the English language.

In one fashion or another, for one reason or another, much of Burke's most enduring discourse served as a form of vindication. Whether he was justifying Rockinghamite policies or his own more personal expressions of political commitment, Burke throughout his life felt obliged to account for himself publicly. The most dramatic and lasting of these efforts came in 1780 when, before the electors of Bristol, he sought to explain his conduct as representative for that very important constituency. The *Speech to the Electors of Bristol* is an exemplary instance of apologiac discourse. Addressing in turn the charges before him—all having to do with his alleged failure to represent adequately the wishes of his city—Burke seized the occasion not only to vindicate his personal conduct, but to present in public a series of reflections on the conduct of political virtue. It is in large part an address on the relationship between virtue and judgment, where judgment is construed to function best in a space between political intimacy and sheer disregard. For many, this is the classic Burke, disdaining the obligations of office and prefiguring his antidemocratic assaults that were to come a decade later. Without entering into that particular debate, I read the speech as a form of rhetorical enactment; Burke is presented as announcing, through the speech act, the conditions of genuine judgment and political virtue. He announces, in short, his discovery of the space of virtue, a realm where judgment is left free to express itself as long as it is justified by reason and the requisites of history.

Of all his many campaigns, Burke believed his attack on Warren Hastings to be, if not the most successful, the most satisfying. Certainly it was his most demanding. For more than a decade Burke led an alternately enthusiastic, fatigued, and finally embarrassed concert of prosecutors against the governor-general of India. Of the countless speeches before Parliament, none was so dramatic, indeed as carnivalesque, as the opening indictments in 1787 before the assembled houses. Carefully orchestrated, contrived to give the prosecutors maximum public visibility and sympathy, the campaign promised to grant Burke a public stage the likes of which he could never command under routine circumstances. The occasion, moreover, gave him an opportunity to dramatize what he believed was an epic clash between virtue and vice. As chief prosecutor, Burke was in a unique position to arrange the terms of his own drama and to write a script within which both he and Hastings were to be viewed as the chief players. Burke, to say the very least, played his part with great enthusiasm; Hastings—for the time at least, and less willingly—

duly played Cataline to Burke's Cicero. Here was an instance, relatively rare for Burke, in which history seemed inclined to promote Burke's vision of political virtue by lending to it the drama of imperial agon.

Finally, and most appropriately, we examine Burke's quite remarkable *Letter to a Noble Lord* (1796). It is one of many efforts to vindicate himself, to reconcile in the public mind his avowed principles of reform and magnanimity before the French Revolution and his seemingly reactionary conservatism after it. But the *Letter* is more than this. It is a riveting attempt by the author to turn the tables on his enemies, to turn defense into attack and to move ultimately to a higher plane of political contest. In many ways it is Burke's most poignant text, shot through with a lifetime's worth of hope and disappointment, of fear, failure, and ambition. The *Letter* reveals a man who, even in the final years before his death, feels more sharply than ever the taunts of his enemies. In addition to being suitable on a personal note, the *Letter* provides us with a final chance to see Burke reworking virtue as a means into history—his own history and that of his country.

These, then, are the texts around which this study is constructed. They are invariably provocative on their own terms, and if my readings can assist those new to Burke or remind those who may have forgotten him, then the modest aim of these essays will have been met. I cannot say whether I have maintained a proper author's distance from my subject. My admiration for Burke is evident; I have chosen not to mask it because I cannot convince myself it is worth concealing. Such admiration is, after all, only the respect accorded to a mind worthy of the effort to understand it.

1

Interpreting Political Culture in the *Present Discontents*

Although we now take the very idea of party politics for granted, it is a relatively recent achievement. Its birth in the eighteenth century was traumatic, its growth marked by controversies both theoretical and practical. At the heart of these disputes was Burke's *Thoughts on the Causes of the Present Discontents* (1770), widely considered the single most important statement on party in its time. Burke's defense of party as a legitimate form of political action represents a turning point in the history of political thought and invites our attention on this basis alone. Because *Discontents* emerged from a heated contest of rival ideas, personalities, and policies, it is equally significant as a rhetorical tract.[1]

Discontents is a long, richly configured, and complex rhetorical text. My reading is designed to show how it can be interpreted as an act of solicitude, made persuasive as the author creates with the reader's participation a relationship of mutual advantage.[2] This analysis focuses on the process by which this relationship is established. In this sense the meaning of Burke's text is not the sum of its recoverable propositions; its meaning, rather, derives from the collaborative experience wherein author and reader reward each other within the terms of the argument itself. This interactive process is identifiable by a series of gestures that direct the rhetorical movement of the text. In the following discussion, I hope to account for this process by demonstrating how Burke creates for his audience an image of itself as virtuous, reminds the reader that virtue is power, and then asks the reader to act in a way consistent with that image by assenting to the argument.

The rhetorical action in Burke's text is its invitation to collaborate in a strategic interpretation of the meaning of political virtue. For Burke, virtue was an expression of enlightened public action, of political will tempered by such values as prudence, right reason, forbearance, magnanimity, order, and collective commitment. Under this rather broad semantic arch, virtue represents for the author a celebration of human community as a medium of historical, religious, economic, and political achievement.[3] As a means of securing this commitment, Burke's argument is appropriately designed to enlist the sympathies of the reader through a kind of "reading-with." It thus requires interpretation of a certain type, neither formal nor exclusively historical, but attentive to the complex process of artistic appeal and informed response. My analysis is therefore grounded, in the words of James Boyd White, in a "reading of a reconstructive and participatory kind, an active engagement with the materials of the text in order to learn about the real or imagined world of which they are a part." In this way, White concludes, "we can establish some sense of the relationship that exists between the speaker and the materials of his culture; that we can experience from the inside, with the intimacy of the artisan, if only in a tentative and momentary way, the life of the language that makes a world."[4] Put another way, Burke's appeal rests on his ability to convince the reader that by interpreting events as he does, together they reclaim virtue by instantiating it.

Rhetorical texts seldom yield to a single, proper reading; not surprisingly, Burke's manifesto of party has stimulated varied and often competing interpretations. Commentators have interpreted it variously: as a thinly veiled and self-interested propaganda piece for the Rockingham Whigs; as a theoretical treatise on the nature of collective political action; as an attack on Chatham's "experiment in heroic, partyless, and patriotic government"; as "an elaborate piece of artifice which might hardly have been recognizable to the very people he was attacking"; and as "a work of political praxis, not theoretical justification."[5]

Whatever the individual merits of these interpretations, collectively they distort Burke's achievement on two scores: they distance appeals to principle and to expedience, and they seriously understate the art by which Burke creates an advantageous relationship with his reader. The analysis presented here moves away from previous readings by closely tracing the shifting contours of Burke's argument and by resisting the temptation to reduce the text to a set of ideological statements.[6] As *Discontents* makes clear, Burke weaves principle and appeal to expediency together so tightly that conventionally antagonistic categories of meaning cannot rent the fabric of his argument. He gives principle the force of self-interest, and self-interest the integrity of principle. The more general aim of this essay is to demonstrate that such a dynamic process is essentially rhetorical; it requires first of all a compelling relationship between author and reader, a mutual understanding of the terms of argument and of how each participant will engage these terms. Burke's stance, in brief, is a posture made forceful only to the extent that an audience is willing to grant it legitimacy. Cajoling an audience into making such a grant can be a difficult task. Here we see how Burke accomplishes it.

The Problem with Parties

"Parties from principle," David Hume observed, "especially abstract speculative principle, are known only to modern times, and are, perhaps, the most extraordinary and unaccountable phenomenon that has yet appeared in human affairs."[7] Hume was not alone in wondering at the emergence of party in his time. In some sense, "party" had been around for most of the century. The term had been used to identify, usually in contentious ways, the dominant Whig/Tory configurations that defined the political landscape. Our understanding of Burke's argument requires that we appreciate the word's pejorative sense. Lord Halifax declared in 1700 "That Parties in a State generally, like Freebooters, hang out False Colours; the pretence is the Publick Good; the real Business is, to catch Prizes; like the Tartars, they presently fall upon the baggage."[8] In fact, with few exceptions, party was for most of the century associated with factional strife, social disruption, and the corruption of public virtue.[9]

The superior alternative, many believed, was given its most complete expression in Bolingbroke's *Idea of a Patriot King* (1749). In voicing the prevailing conception of party, Bolingbroke's tract held parties to be inherently and inevitably a kind of social curse; not only were parties evil, they were avoidable, and could be excluded from political life by granting to the Crown superordinate powers. The patriot king, Bolingbroke wrote, "far from forming or espousing a party" rather will "defeat party in defence of the Constitution, on some occasions; and lead men, from acting with a party spirit, to act with a national spirit, in others."[10] With the breakdown of Whig orthodoxy, the fading of the Jacobite threat, and the fragmentation of the political scene after 1760, however, Bolingbroke's ideal world-without-party seemed more elusive than ever. Nevertheless, George

III's announced antipathy to party politics remained for many an appealing commitment.

The Rockingham Whigs were a proprietary party of wealthy landowners and erstwhile officeholders. Almost in spite of themselves, the group commanded some of the best talent in a crowded political arena. As head of government from July 1765 to July of the following year, the Rockingham ministry had directed the overturn of Grenville's much-abused Stamp Act and had thereby gained some measure of affection from both the English merchants and their colonial counterparts. But while their principles could be at times inspired, their politics were not strong enough to withstand pressures from the Crown and from competing coalitions. Back in opposition, the Rockinghamites continued to face on the one side an antipathetic court and on the other a volatile series of coalition ministries. Thus confronted, the Rockingham group feared for its political identity and so welcomed the tireless assistance of the marquis's secretary.[11] In Edmund Burke they found a propagandist who promised to offset the political lethargy that had beset the party.

Burke's task was clearly a difficult one. He was expected not only to revitalize the dispirited Rockinghamites, but also to confront the political legacy of the 1760s. The prospect was more formidable because he could count on so few certainties. A long period of relative stability under Walpole and the Old Corps was at an end, its hegemony destroyed with the ascent of George III in 1760. The new decade ushered in a host of disputes. Among these were controversies over constitutional authority; fears that too much power was being delivered into the hands of the king and his "friends"; fear that the people were seizing undue influence over the affairs of the nation; the ongoing series of ministries, some lasting little more than a year; the influence of a secret cabal on the judgment of king and ministers; and the Wilkes affair and its attending issues of Parliamentary authority and constraint. All these issues overlapped in various ways, and together they presented to Burke a formidable rhetorical problem.[12]

Above all, Burke had to refocus the fading identity of his party. In addition to Rockingham's desultory leadership, the combination was threatened by the emergence of rival parties and competing leadership, most notably that of Shelbourne, Grenville, Townshend, and North. Late in 1769 Burke wrote to Rockingham of his anxiety to show "the ground upon which the Party stands; and how different its Constitution, as well as the persons who compose it are from the Bedfords, and Grenvilles, and other knots, who are combined for no Publik purpose; but only as a means of furthering with joint strength, their private and individual advantage."[13] To a significant degree these groups were appealing not so much on the basis of their political creed as "Whigs" as by their ability to seize actual power. As *Discontents* makes clear, Burke saw this as a challenge to the integrity of his party and set out to reconcile the dictates of principle with those of political action.

If on one side Burke faced the protean force of coalition politics, on the other he faced the renegade leadership of William Pitt, Lord Chatham. Fiercely independent, unpredictable, and at times unstable, Chatham struggled now to retain his power as he never had before. Unquestionably he was the most popular leader of his time: he was an unrivaled orator, an extremely cunning politician, and a hugely successful war minister. But Chatham had wearied many supporters with the expensive war between 1757 and 1763. As the Great Commoner he had gambled recklessly with public opinion by accepting a pension in 1763 and, worse still, a peerage in 1766. Even his thundering speeches were beginning to sound hollow and less impressive. But, as even King George understood, Chatham could not be disregarded, and he managed to recapture the ministry after the fall of Rockingham. However, under Grafton's nominal leadership and Chatham's brooding presence, the coalition ministry soon splintered badly. Out of power again, Chatham threatened to spirit away party supporters under his charismatic leadership and his pronouncements of "measures, not men." Chatham's politics were paradoxical, heroic, and outdated, but they posed a serious threat to Burke's sense of party loyalty.[14]

The court was another factor. Burke and many others had long believed that the king was being unduly influenced by a small group of private advisors.[15] This court faction, referred to variously as the "King's Friends," "double cabinet," or simply the "cabal," was initially led by the notorious Lord Bute. Even after Bute's ostensible fall in 1763, many alleged that his insidious presence could be readily invoked, and his power continued to the decade's end. As a conspiratorial figure, Bute could not have been more fitting; physically unattractive, politically dense, unaccountably powerful, he was at once to be loathed and feared. Now little historical evidence supports the claim that Bute's influence was as great as many believed. Calling forth his image in 1770 was, even then, stretching the conspiracy a bit far. For this reason perhaps, Burke was anxious in *Discontents* to exploit the rhetorical force of hidden influence as a "system" rather than as the instigations of an individual, even one so tempting as Lord Bute. As an inventive resource, the threat of a secret power at work against the Constitution provided Burke with a valuable means to contrast his own party's openness, its principled politics, and its claim on the support of the virtuous public.[16] To accomplish this, he had to recast public attitudes toward the idea of party itself.

Interpreting Political Culture

Burke's task was to capture and recast the symbolic power of party. If, as he thought, the Rockinghamites were strongest as they were united, and if unity—especially in opposition—was conventionally held in suspicion, then he had to articulate a rationale for party that went well beyond self-interest. In this sense *Discontents* can be seen as serving a variety of purposes; these purposes in turn structure the argument and lend to it an inescapably pragmatic spirit. The early moments of the text situate author and reader in an interpretive relationship and distinguish the proper grounds for political critique. The second phase nurtures this relationship by assuring the reader that assent to the argument constitutes an act of virtue. And the final phase celebrates the relationship by calling to action those who understand as the author and reader now understand.

In light of this complex of purposes, labeling *Discontents* either as philosophy or as a mere political tract distorts its rhetorical character. Burke required a set of principles to order and make plausible his rhetorical purposes; he needed to construe those rhetorical purposes to give his principles theoretical force. This reading of Burke's argument suggests that in virtue he found a means to unify these needs.

"Eighteenth-century England," J. C. D. Clark writes, "was not an oriental despotism: the public, its interests, its judgements, and its aspirations, mattered intensely. But they mattered practically in so far as, and in the ways in which, they were brought into the political arena by politicians."[17] Burke's potential readership was composed of just this volatile mix of politicians and the public. To move them, he had to provide first a rationale for action, thereby to set in motion the first phases of this argument. The reader exercises an option either to take up Burke's challenge or to stop reading. The introduction begins this persuasive process.

In cases of tumult and disorder, our law has invested every man, in some sort, with the authority of a magistrate. When the affairs of the nation are distracted, private people are, by the spirit of that law, justified in stepping out of their ordinary sphere. They enjoy a privilege, of somewhat more dignity and effect, than that of idle lamentation over the calamities of their country. They may look into them narrowly; they may reason upon them liberally; and if they should be so fortunate as to discover the true source of the mischief, and to suggest any probable method of removing it, though they may displease the rulers for the day, they are certainly of service to the cause of government.

By stressing the virtue of political action, the author gives his request a moral incentive; by reminding the reader of the power of the individual voice, Burke encourages confident resolve. Thus he posits an ideal reader and invites his actual audience to become this ideal.[18] This strategy is, no doubt, old-fashioned flattery, but more important, the remarks locate "the people" (the reader) as the authorizing source of legitimate political action.[19]

No one, neither himself nor others, then or now, would mistake Burke's gesture to the people as much more than just that. But his recourse to public power was not necessarily disingenuous. For rhetorical purposes, it underscores the collaborative relationship between author and reader; Burke in effect empowers the reader as a critic and, hence, provides an incentive to secure the relationship. "Nations are governed by the same methods," Burke writes, "and on the same principles, by which an individual without authority is often able to govern those who are his equals or superiors; by a knowledge of their temper, and by a judicious management of it."

Beyond simple ingratiation then, Burke's introduction works crucially to determine the proper relationship between author, reader, and interpretive task. In his role as the reader's representative, Burke understands well that "the temper of the people amongst whom he presides ought therefore to be the first study of a statesman." As it is with the statesman, so Burke would have it with the critic of political culture.

Having justified the act of criticism and defined its essential structure, Burke pushes the argument forward by distinguishing its proper ground. As with much of Burke's public discourse, this process is driven by a discriminating impulse, an effort to discuss what is legitimate as an object of criticism and what is not. Here we see Burke instructing the reader, newly welcomed into the political fold: "To complain of the age we live in, to murmur at the present possession of power, to lament the past, to conceive extravagant hopes of the future, are the common dispositions of the greatest part of mankind; indeed the necessary effect of the ignorance and levity of the vulgar." This much, Burke suggests, is not especially interesting or productive as a mode of inquiry; rather, "true political sagacity manifests itself in distinguishing that complaint which only characterizes the general infirmity of human nature, from those which are symptom of the particular distemperature of our own air and season."

When Burke proceeds to discuss this "particular distemperature," he encourages the reader to see in him just such a "political sagacity," and it is a kind of political wisdom he is eager to share. Burke is quick and he is deft; but the strategic deference to the reader in which he couches his argument is evident. To those who attribute the present disorder to a combination of imperial wealth and a volatile people, Burke responds with a series of reductive arguments exposing the fallacy of blaming the people, not government. Such a position, he notes, will imply "That we have a very good ministry, but that we are a very bad people." This position Burke will not tolerate, and he shows himself to be at pains to refute it. At this earlier point in the text, Burke is still tying the bonds of intimacy with his reader; as they become tighter, his otherwise incredible claims seem more secure.

Burke's "political sagacity," we come to see, embraces his community of readers as well as his object of inquiry. Thus his depiction of popular authority is strategic: deferring to it at some points, at others straining to clarify his intention and its limits. "I am not one of those," he writes, "who think that the people are never in the wrong. They have been so, frequently and outrageously, both in other countries and in this." Burke is quick, however, to balance this assessment with the more encouraging judgment: "But I do say, that in all disputes between them and their rulers, the presumption [of political rectitude] is at least upon a par in favor of the people." Ultimately, Burke concludes, "The people have no interest in disorder. When they do wrong it is their error and not their crime. But with the governing part of the state it is far otherwise. They may certainly act ill by design, as well as by mistake."

As the title of this work makes plain, Burke is searching for a cause. In going to the reader for help, Burke reveals the text for what it is: an argument. Burke's appeal to the virtues of public action requires that the reader agree to his terms: that he lead, the reader follow, and in this way discover the true causes of the present discontents. Presumably, such an arrangement will give to the reader powers of revelation and judgment unrealized before.

"It is very rare indeed for men to be wrong in their feelings concerning public misconduct; as rare to be right in their speculation upon the cause of it." For this reason, Burke intimates, "there are but very few who are capable of comparing and digesting what passes before their eyes at different times and occasions, so as to form the whole into a distinct system." Imagining who Burke has in mind here is not difficult, and we are assured of the author's implied role as the passage progresses. These reflections on the limits of historical reasoning, moreover, provide a crucial transition in the text from its introductory moments to its narrative phases. Having taught us our roles and responsibilities, Burke educates the reader now on how to think and, more specifically, how not to think.

For Burke and for Burke's reader, the times are portentous, and they can be interpreted only with the greatest caution. By inviting the reader to participate in an act of political interpretation, by explaining that such participation is actually a form of virtuous public action, by delineating the proper roles and grounds of interpretive authority, Burke has arranged for a collaborative investigation into the causes of the present discontents. Anticipating the strain on our credibility and his credence, Burke casts the reader as he would cast his electorate: willing, obliged, deferential, and anxious for results. Here is a form of "practiced friendship" Burke will, by his own reckoning, have cause to celebrate.

Reading Conspiracy

Whatever success Burke has achieved in capturing the credulity of his reader is quickly put to the test. As by far the longest and most developed argument in the text, the narrative details an insidious history of court design. It is, in effect, an exercise in reading conspiracy; the author labors to expose concerted evil while the reader is asked to grant credence where the pleasures of revelation are greatest. There was nothing particularly novel about this rhetoric of conspiracy; it had been a part of the political landscape since the ascendency of Bute a decade earlier. If anything, Burke was trying to revitalize what many thought to be a dead concern. But the force of his argument indicates that Burke understood the appeal to conspiracy as a rhetorical form. He understood that once it is underway, as Bernard Bailyn has written, "it could not be easily dispelled: denial only confirmed it, since what conspirators profess is not what they believe; the ostensible is not real; and the real is deliberately maligned."[20] In the hands of Burke, such a rhetorical resource could be used to powerful effect indeed.

Coming fast on the heels of an attack on facile historicity, Burke's narrative of conspiracy can seem inconsistent at best. Burke is substituting one history for another, and as he exploits a lurid curiosity in the reader, he undermines orthodox readings of contemporary events. He is able to do this because, like most narratives, his story highlights historical coherence and direction. Burke's own plot, moreover, gives to his narrative the sense of being better able to account for the full sweep and complexity of events. It provides, in short, a superior order, a form which the author can superimpose upon the "furious disorder" of current affairs. And if we recall Burke's earlier complaint that few are able to discern with any accuracy the sweep of present events, we can better anticipate Burke's own privileged role as he undertakes his story of hidden motives, dark design, and unscrupulous men.

Burke begins at some point before the revolution and weaves his story within a pattern of constitutional fate. He is most concerned to detail the growth of court influence, which he claims had returned in the decade of the 1760s with unprecedented power. The courtiers had then worked quickly. While the new monarch was enjoying a very brief period of national quiet, the court was plotting to restore its secret influence over Crown and country. They proceeded, Burke explains, "to destroy everything of strength which did not derive its principle nourishment from the immediate pleasures of the court." Their first victim was William Pitt, and then the other great political families; before long, the court had managed to dissolve any connection with the people, whether expressed through the independency of Pitt or the landed Whig proprietors. Through all their dealings, the "great ruling principle of the cabal, and that which animated and harmonized all their proceedings, was to signify to the world that the court would proceed upon its own forces only."

The remaining narrative is an extended interplay between the "facts" of the conspiracy—its sources, agents, motives, and effects— and its implications for public virtue. It is a prolonged argument, detailed and complex. Out of this interplay emerges a more general set of claims that help define the public character of the text. For every instance of destruction wrought by the cabal, Burke poses against it a standard of right action. Thus Burke condemns the court faction, not on the basis of individual (i.e., Bute's) behavior, but as a system. And systems, the author insists, threaten because they cannot be held accountable. Individuals are visible, systems are not, Burke argues. Thus systems need to justify their power to popular will. Consequently, he adds, "No conveniency of public arrangement is available to remove any one of them from the specific situation he holds; and the slightest attempt upon one of them, be he the most powerful minister, is a certain preliminary to his own destruction."

In what is perhaps the most condensed and forceful of these expressions, Burke now steps back to reflect on the prerequisites of legitimate political power. As the reader will have come to expect by this point, the reflection underscores both his attack on the secret cabal and confirms the author's ongoing commitment to the reader's welfare. Burke accomplishes the task through neither a novel conception of government nor even a particularly new interpretation of representative government. Rather, Burke carefully asserts a simple series of constitutional and cultural commonplaces. He does so, however, in such a compact and forceful way, that their rhetorical appeal remains alive: "Before men are put forward into the great trusts of the state, they ought by their conduct to have obtained such a degree of estimation in their country, as may be some sort of pledge and security to the public, that they will not abuse those trusts. It is no mean security for a proper use of power, that a man has shown by the general tenor of his actions, that the affection, the good opinion, the confidence of his fellow-citizens have been among the principle objects of his life." For this reason among others, the court faction and the influence it wields are unconstitutional. Without such public trust, without being held to account by the judgment of the people, the court faction forfeits any real claim to legitimate power. Such men, Burke concludes, "ought never to be suffered to domineer in the state; because they have no connection with the sentiments and opinions of the people."

These repeated gestures to the people serve Burke's rhetorical purposes well. They provide a means to contrast the activities of his political enemies and to dramatize their disruptive influence on the fortunes of his reader. Repeatedly, he returns to questions of public virtue and its relationship to political power. These gestures, aside from fueling the adversarial force of Burke's narrative, also work to sustain the author's relationship with the reader. In effect Burke reminds his audience that as the ultimate victims of this cabal, the reader must acknowledge its presence and act with Burke to destroy it.

Even as Burke recounts this story of corruption in high places, he never allows the reader to lose sight of virtue itself. Burke magnifies the cabalistic threat to the political culture of his reader to the point of enormity. As his audience reads these lines, the readers realize portents of their own destruction. The prose itself reflects the heat of danger and the immediacy of the threat; it is pointed, rapid, angry. As the court factions prevail, Burke warns, "A sullen gloom and furious disorder prevails by fits; the nation loses its relish for peace and prosperity. . . . A species of men to whom a state of order would become a sentence of obscurity are nourished into a dangerous magnitude by the heat of intestine disturbances; and it is no wonder that, by a sort of sinister society, they cherish, in their turn, the disorders which are the parents of all their consequence."

The final moments of Burke's argument are vivid, but they are not isolated. His discussion of party, considered a classic statement on the character of political association, is typically treated as distinct, as if it could somehow retain its full range of meanings extrapolated from the preceding argument. In fact, such an approach is unwarranted. More than a set piece on the advantages of political party, the conclusion of *Discontents* represents a cumulative phase; it could be nowhere else in the text without loss of meaning and effect. How we understand the message, then, is very much a matter of understanding its relationship to the rest of the text.

Up to this point Burke has skillfully integrated general precepts with specific examples, a tactic typical of his rhetorical practice. Here, on the other hand, Burke pulls away from his moorings and seems more ready to indulge his theoretical interests in the nature of party action. The key to the argument's success and meaning is that this section deploys what has been achieved so far: a relationship between author and reader elastic enough to grant these extended claims and yet retain its basis in mutual trust. Everything up to this part serves the final argument. All depictions—the conspiracies, the case study in political abuse, the "furious disorder" of the government—function as warrants for the author's final declaration in defense of party and the public it serves and by which it is served.

Burke's transition into the final phase makes evident to the reader the argument's essential logic. If the cabal is evil, the people act to destroy its influence; and since the people are best served by party representation, they lend the legitimacy of public virtue to party (i.e., the Rockinghamites). Thus Burke reminds the reader again of that virtue as well as its proper exercise. At this stage in the argument, since Burke can count on the reader's sympathy, he is eager to exercise it to the advantage of both public and party. Moving now to his treatment of party, Burke can challenge that sympathy, confident that his implied meanings will not go astray. "Government may in a great measure be restored," Burke confides, "if any considerable bodies of men have honesty and resolution enough never to accept administration, when this garrison of King's men, which is stationed, as in a citadel, to control and enclose it be entirely broken and disbanded, and every work they leave thrown up be levelled with the ground."

Out of the ruins, Burke argues, emerge principles of ordered and public government. These principles are best expressed in and through party. However, Burke does not ignore the power of his enemies. Accordingly he initiates the defense of party by refuting the antiparty line. Burke is, in effect, protecting his reader; by exposing to them the false rhetoric of the cabal, he dramatizes the claim of his own party to the public interest. The cabal, Burke warns, professes to believe that "all political connections are in their nature factious and as such ought to be dissipated and destroyed." Burke's account of why the court figures should promote this line of attack is circular; but like many such arguments, however, the explanation is effective. The cabal abuses party, Burke explains, because "whilst men are linked together, they easily and speedily communicate the alarm of any evil design. They are enabled to fathom it with common counsel, and to oppose it with united strengths." This parallel between the responsibilities of the people and the motives to party is deliberate; by it Burke manages to construe yet again his ideal standard of political action. Called upon to redress governmental failures, the people respond by supporting those who, in their position of party strength, can effect the proper remedies. Ultimately, Burke writes, this rationale is plain to all: "When bad men combine, the good must associate; else they will fall, one by one, an unpitied sacrifice in a contemptible struggle."

Within the contour of Burke's argument, this line of argument has become a recurrent pattern. Author and reader now expect the insidious design of the king's friends to destroy party, but author and reader know that party is the only form of political action capable of bringing down their artifice. Evil prefers disorder and the weakness that inevitably attends it; party represents order and strength. This reasoning gives the political actor a moral imperative to act. Merely conceding the necessity of party or enduring it at the level of principle is not sufficient. Rather, the individual who commands virtue will not only consent to the advantages of party and act, but unite with others. Such united action is the only way to make principle meaningful. Public duty, he reasons, "demands and requires, that what is right should not only be made known, but made prevalent; that what is evil should not only be detected, but defeated." Burke concludes, "It is surely no very rational account of a man's life, that he has always acted right, but has taken special care, to act in such a manner that his endeavors could not possibly be productive of any consequence."

Burke does not usually write of essences, and when he does, some kind of history follows. This characteristic move ensures access to the argument by giving the reader a way to embody and witness conceptual abstraction. For Burke, the turn to history also illustrates how the principle remains intact despite "accidental" failings. First, he turns to the Roman republic. Here he finds his idea of party celebrated by great patriots who looked upon political connection "with a sacred reverence." This allusion is more than convenient; it allows him to affirm and illustrate the idea and to show readers that they are participating in a relationship of enduring power. Thus Burke elaborates on the Roman experience by isolating the precondition of party/public virtue. As with us, he says, the great patriots of old "believed private honor to be the great foundation of public trust; that friendship was no mean step towards patriotism; that he who, in the common intercourse of life, showed he regarded somebody besides himself, when he came to act on a public situation, might probably consult some interest other than his own."

"Friendship" emerges as a principle that both underlies and embraces the conduct of virtue and fuses the public and private by conjoining the sentiments of fraternity with the requisites of community. The principle, we now recognize, extends to the text itself, where the rhetorical effect is contingent on just such a "practiced friendship." The public character of the argument is given its full range of meaning and effect in the privacy of its reading. Hence what Burke describes as an ancient belief in political association may be taken as a standard of rhetorical concert. "It was their wish," he writes, "to see public and private virtues, not dissonant and jarring, and mutually destructive, but harmoniously combined, growing out of one another in a noble and orderly gradation, reciprocally supporting and supported."

Having delayed any precise definition of party to this point, Burke offers to the reader a direct proposition. He has refuted competing claims on the credulity of his reader; he has given the force of history to his justification of party; and he has, yet again, grounded the reader's expectations in the same virtues constituting the principle of party. Burke's definition is, in a word, safe. It comes just a few pages short of the end and is thus buttressed by one hundred pages of carefully wrought argument. And it is quite simple: "Party is a body of men united for promoting by their joint endeavors the national interest upon some particular principle in which they are all agreed."

But although simple, the definition in effect carries the weight of the entire argument; it has been, in a sense, achieved, earned through the joint labor of reader and writer. We note, especially, the stress on Burke's favorite commonplaces: party, unity, action, nation, and principle. Each of these values has been exercised recurrently in the progress of the text so far, and as they are here offered in the form of a definition, they come to represent and reflect the very sense they are designed to express.

Put another way, the definition is itself stated as an expression of enlightened political action. Burke has shown himself to be acting as an unabashed party spokesman, has sought not only to defend such unity but also to create it with his readers, and has promoted the definition as a vital principle conducive to the welfare of his country. This done, Burke's reader need not be confused as to the implied reference in his famous dictum: "It is the business of the speculative philosopher to mark the proper end of government. It is the business of the politician who is the philosopher in action to find out proper means towards these ends, and to employ them with effect."

That Burke thought of himself as a philosopher in action is something of a truism.[21] Certainly no other politician during the last half of the century gave such sustained attention to ideas as Burke. And yet like most truisms, it does not actually tell us much; most often it serves as a reminder to those who would limit Burke's contributions to the exclusive domain of philosophy. Of course, the reminder is useful, but we may ignore the more interesting question of how Burke presents himself as a philosopher in action. By this point, Burke has enacted that role for many pages. Among other advantages, this process allows him to confront his most formidable challenge, rhetorical and political, in the character of Chatham.

As the Great Commoner, Chatham's presence was substantial and enigmatic; his professions of independence directly threatened Burke's claim to party virtue. Burke has just celebrated the virtues of political connection at the level of definition and principle; now he confronts the immediate problem of Chatham in the terms afforded by that discussion. Thus Burke characterizes Chatham's phrase "Not men but measures" as "a sort of charm by which people get loose from every honorable engagement." When the politician acts independent of party, Burke reminds the reader, he may be acting honorably; but, he writes, "I lament to see qualities, rare and valuable, squandered away without any public utility." The more pressing issue, however, regards those who (Burke declines to name Chatham) make political currency out of these dubious professions.[22]

To act independent of party, Burke argues, is to act alone and, thus, invisibly. Conversely, "When people desert this connection, the desertion is a manifest fact, upon which a direct simple inner lair, triable by plain men." In this way, Burke casts the weight of Chathamite principle against the weight of his own argument for public virtue and political accountability. Acting alone, far from being a mark of courage, draws a justifiable suspicion for violating the conditions of political community. The clear implication here is that both the cabal and Pitt are culpable on this score: attaining and exercising power under conditions of privation, they are outside the political standards of public virtue.

Burke effectively frames his depiction of Chatham's principles with a litany of his own. The lines are an argument driven to its final end by principle. The conclusion issues a set of moral imperatives designed to give virtue its most compelling rationale. Burke's reader, in any case, must now confront the consequences of these contending principles: "If other ideas should prevail," Burke concludes, "things must remain in their present confusion, until they are hurried into all the rage of civil violence, or until they reach into the dead repose of despotism."

Conclusion

Burke's *Discontents* can be meaningfully read as an instantiation of political virtue. To the extent that it represents a public, persuasive argument, it participates in political controversy; it demands action of a particular kind, the elements of which are defined and promoted in the text itself. Within its pattern of arguments and appeals, a standard of political virtue emerges that is both constituted and acted upon in the progress of the text. This conception of virtue can be expressed as a form of concerted action, made public and accountable, and accrued to the benefit of the political community.

The rhetorical action of the text is the process by which this conception is given force. Burke's argument is cumulative; it constantly banks on itself to drive the claims forward until, at its conclusion, all preceding claims are given coherence and persuasive effect. For Burke to achieve his ends, he must establish a certain relationship with his reader. That created relationship provides the authoritative ground for Burke's discourse; he patiently nurtures his readers not only in how to read the text, but about why they should read and be persuaded by it. If convinced, the reader becomes, in effect, a warrant to the author's argument.

Interpreting an author who is in turn asking us to perceive as he does situates our own work in a distinctive way and reminds us again of the eternal loop that unites modern readers with historical texts.[23] This reading of Burke's text is offered as a plausible alternative to the extrapolation of principles familiar to the historian of ideas.[24] If, as with Burke's text, the language is compelling enough, we become signified by its terms; we become both interpreters and interpreted. This interplay of referents dissolves pretensions to sheer objectivity and stresses, instead, the possibility of embracing distant texts within the horizons of our own understanding.

2

Reading Virtue and Rhetorical Portraiture in the *Speech on Taxation*

If Burke's *Discontents* has a great deal to say about the structure of virtue, it is remarkable too for the way in which it fills in that structure with personality and psychological insight. Such grounding of principle in lived experience will become characteristic of Burke's discourse of virtue; it is indeed part of his legacy as a political theorist and party polemicist. We may date the origins of this habit of art and mind to the decade of the 1770s, when Burke's star was rising and his opportunities for public expression were expanding rapidly. Perhaps no more forceful example of how the concept of virtue gets embodied in human form can be found than in Burke's 1774 *Speech on Taxation*. An address of considerable length and complexity, it is among other things an important reminder that virtue is ultimately an attribute of character. And while virtuous character is fully realized only as it is beheld—made public and servicable—it remains explicable only as it is, quite literally, embodied. On this premise, Burke's oration is important for two reasons: it exemplifies the process by which virtue is grounded in character and thus given rhetorical force, and it provides a means by which the reader can learn to read virtue in the face of those who possess it.

Of Burke's major orations, the *Speech on Taxation* is among the most difficult to appreciate. However vaguely, critics and historians are nonetheless inclined to grant it a central place in the canon of Burke's performances.[1] To the rhetorical critic specifically, the speech is impressive for its mastery of detail, reasoning, and force of argument. It is not, perhaps for these very traits, an easy work to read. Long, intricate, rigorous, the speech demands from the reader a degree of concentration and patience seldom extended on behalf of political oratory. Still, if we can figure out a way to read the text as Burke invites us to read it, then the pain of interpretation diminishes, even disappears. Far from an elaborate exercise in tedium, reading *Taxation* can yield a surprising number of insights into Burke's artistry and his command of the oration as a rhetorical form. It is, by extension of these considerations, highly suggestive as an example of how he generally conceived the relationship between politics and virtue.

In what was a pattern for Burke's speeches, the address was met with varied degrees of enthusiasm. Burke had, of course, been speaking in Commons for almost a decade, but the speech may well have launched his fame as an orator. Reporters for *Parliamentary History* noted that on its conclusion, Burke "was allowed to have excelled himself, and to have made one of the most masterly speeches that was ever uttered in a public assembly." Horace Walpole, as we might expect, qualified his judgment of the performance, but the begrudging respect is there. "The redundancy of images," Walpole confided, "the pursuit of wit, even to puerility, the want of judgment and sobriety, and the still greater want of art to touch the passions, rank this great composition (which was the greater, as it was spoken unpremeditated) but with the species of imperfect eloquence."[2]

That the *Speech on Taxation* should come to represent Burke's unusual and early command of historical detail and economic issues is perhaps not surprising. The argument is informed in ways that his audience had never known, and the sheer accumulation of detail can be overwhelming. But audiences do not, as did Lord Townshend upon hearing the speech, shout "Heavens! What a man this is! Where could he acquire such transcendent powers!" over history lessons and financial briefs.[3] Burke's first great oration, rather, made its claim not because it was learned, though learned it was, but because it so powerfully wove into the fabric of history the multicolored threads of human agency and personality.

The *Speech on Taxation* advances its meaning and secures its force on two levels of signification. The first and most obvious level can be recognized as narrative in form and function; the second involves a gallery of character portraits. Burke is, as we have come to expect in his discourse, telling a story, and in fact, he uses the very word repeatedly to describe his efforts and aims. Though it is exacting, its course is a readily discernible, even predictable review of Anglo-colonial relations from the Restoration to the eve of war with America. Integrated into this narrative is a review of six character sketches; these portraits, I suggest, are the keys to reading the speech. Punctuating and shaping the text, these character portraits include the likes of Grenville, Rockingham, Conway, Burke himself, Chatham, and Townshend. What tasks do these portraits perform, what is their relationship to the narrative progress of *Taxation*, and what do they have to say about character and virtue as rhetorical constructs?

Rhetorical Portraiture

While these questions can only be answered in the process of our reading, we may begin with a few possibilities. As rhetorical technique, the character portraits in effect seize the action of the narrative; by interpolating its progression, they shift the signifying process from narrative action to an interpretive space for reflection. Nothing "moves" in these portraits; they are fixed and certain. They function as dwelling points, hermeneutic sites, and call attention to their rhetorical status in the text by digressing from its dominant mode of expression. The character portraits provide a space for reflective judgment; and as they concern character—public character— they invite the reader into the text in a way that the more technical aspects of the narrative cannot. Hence they function as interpretive keys; they give to the reader a means to make sense of the complex and taxing narrative. To the extent that we find Burke's portraits convincing, they are constituted as warrants for believing the claims embedded in the narrative proper. The portraits are thus, in the words of Dennis Bormann, an "organic part of the argument because they embody the argument and set it before the eyes of the audience." By extension, then, "these pictures are not passages which distract from Burke's argument; indeed," Bormann insists, "they serve a functional purpose since they actually portray or embody the argument."[4] Burke thus deploys two different modes of inducement— for believing in character is different than believing in narrative proof—and weaves them into the rich fabric of the oration.

This approach to the text, furthermore, adjusts conventional approaches to ethos as a rhetorical proof. The portraits work by creating and dramatizing, by making rhetorically engaging, the character of others, not ostensibly the author. They accordingly deflect attention from the author's character as a disputable basis for proof and toward the more easily designed and controlled character fabricated in the rhetorical text. By "reading" them, the audience is better able to read the "objective" events represented in the narrative.

Here is virtue created through the text and in the eyes of the author; it is a rhetorical construct, informed by epideictic conventions of praise and blame. And like epideictic rhetoric, it plays off of, requires, engages, and affirms public values. This enterprise in the creation of virtue cannot at these key moments afford risk, for risk will come in the narrative argument. It demands the certainties of epideictic as a foundation upon which this argument must work.

Analysis of the Text

On 28 March 1774 permission was given to bring before the House of Commons a bill for "the better regulating the Government of the Province of Massachusetts Bay, in North America." Given the state of Anglo-American relations at that time, many thought the bill overdue, to say the very least. A bit more than two weeks later, Rose Fuller, M.P. for Rye, moved for the following: "That at this House will, upon this day seven-night, resolve itself into a committee of the whole House, to take into consideration the duty of 3d per pound weight upon tea, payable in all his Majesty's dominion in America, imposed by the said Act; and also the appropriation of the said duty." Fuller thus set in motion a debate of unusual duration, if not intensity, and gave to Burke an occasion ripe for his own display. By the time he rose to his feet, the House was by all accounts weary. Soon, however, reports "of what was going on spread in every quarter," and as Burke spoke on, "members came crowding back, till the hall was filled to the utmost, and resounded throughout the speech with the loudest expressions of applause." Burke, perhaps sensing its importance, immediately had the speech set in type—his first such request.[5]

Burke initiates the speech with a lament. For nearly a decade, he notes, the House has been occupied with colonial policy, and yet little has been done to remedy the ongoing series of crises. The introductory remarks, however, involve more than simple complaint. Burke, typically, takes advantage of these early moments to reflect on the nature and progress of these deliberations. The House has been, he declares, "lashed round and round this miserable circle of occasional argument and temporary expedients. I am sure our heads must turn and our stomachs nauseate with them. We have had them in every shape; we have looked at them in every point of view. Invention is exhausted; reason is fatigued; experience has given judgment; but obstinacy is not yet conquered."

Burke's depiction of Parliament's mode of proceeding is the first of many similar charges, and it hints at a recurrent theme in the speech.

Time and again he will attack the Ministry's "miserable circle of occasional arguments and temporary expedients" as exemplary of faulty deliberation. This negative characterization in turn sets up its positive counterpart, e.g., the Rockingham program. Hence the first few paragraphs give relatively abstract expression to the speaker's general argument; later, he will embody these terms in their respective spokesman.

As to Cornwall's suggestion that "the only proper subject of inquiry is not how we got into this difficulty, but how we are to get out of it," Burke is adamant. He takes the occasion to elaborate on his own mode of deliberation and, consequently, to set in relief his rhetorical judgment from that of his disputant. "In other words," Burke reasons, "we are, according to him, to consult our invention, and to reject our experience. The mode of deliberation he recommends is deemed diametrically opposite to every rule of reason and every principle of good sense established among mankind."

Burke's introductory remarks thus serve notice that the speech is as much about political reasoning as about conclusions drawn. His argument is in this sense double-layered: it seeks not only to displace the policies of his opposition, but also to reconstitute what the speaker believes to be a legitimate process of deliberation. This double-layering creates a mirroring effect, where arguments draw attention to themselves as either affirming Burke's deliberative standards or as violating them; in either case, we can see throughout the ensuing narrative a continual interplay between reflections on political reason and more explicit assertions of deliberative policy. As Burke moves into the first of his historical reviews, he offers a concrete example of this process. Promising to anchor his claims in a verifiable past, Burke announces that it is "to that experience, without the least wavering or hesitation on my part, I steadily appeal; and would to God there was no other arbiter to decide on the vote with which the House is to conclude this day."

The experience to which Burke alludes will serve his argument well. As he undertakes a retrospective on the career of colonial relations, the various acts and their repeal emerge as inductive proof for his argument; hence, he refutes the charge that Rockingham's repeal of this Stamp Act invited colonial contempt and contends that, in fact, the Townshend duties were to blame for perpetuating American grievances. As his counterarguments mount, Burke generates a series of refutations designed to expose ministerial folly and to reveal government claims to acting on principle as disingenuous. In particular, Burke attacks the preamble to the Act of 1767, which announces England's right to tax the colonies for revenue. As five-sixth of the taxes had since been repealed, Burke found the principles of right declared in the preamble pointless. The current Ministry's recourse to it was therefore "an empty, absurd, false recital." The preamble was no reason to prevent repeal of the final duty on tea, and those who defended the duty on that ground, Burke argued, confused the proper distinction between principle and expedience.

For Burke, good politics was a matter of seeing things rightly. The virtuous statesman was one who could encourage particulars within an orderly system and yet not lose sight of those particulars or insist too rigidly on the application of that system. By characterizing the Ministry as lacking this kind of political virtue, Burke sets up the means to contrast North's administration against Rockingham's opposition. Immediately following his attack on the particular issues involved, Burke in effect contemplates the general cause of the current crisis. His most damning charge, indeed, issues from the reflection that "nothing in the world can read so awful and so instructive a lesson, as the conduct of ministry in their business upon the mischief of not having large and liberal ideas in the management of great affairs." The problem, Burke contends, was that government leaders lacked perspective; they had not "looked at the whole of your complicated interests in one connected view." Instead, the speaker reasons, they have "taken things bits by scraps, some at one time and one pretense, and some at another . . . they never had any kind of system right or wrong, but only invented occasionally some miserable tale for the day, in order meanly to sneak out of difficulties into which they had proudly strutted."

Although still early in the speech, we already become aware of recurrent images, metaphors, and phrases. They prove to be the stock of Burke's oration, the figurative vocabulary that shapes his ideas and gives them force. They are, as well, meaningful as modes of implication; thus North's ministry is marked by a "miserable circle" of arguments, its deliberations nauseate, exhaust, hesitate, and waver. Burke suggests, conversely, that he acts and has acted in accordance to rules of right reason and with experience, principles of good sense, steadiness, system, and enlarged perspective. These attributes and their counterparts will converge and become embodied as descriptions of political virtue generally. Steady, grounded, directed, rational, and enlightened: this is Burke's ideal statesman, the standard against which he will judge others.

Having exposed the partisan aims behind the repeal of the Stamp Act—and its refusal to repeal the tax on tea—Burke badgers the Ministry with relentless detail. Forcing the issue, revealing inconsistencies, presenting his documents and letters, Burke labors to add weight and strength to his argument. The effect, in part, is to contrast again his own manner of proceeding against the rhetorical action of his enemies. Whereas Burke has conspicuously developed a substantial and direct assault on the Ministry, North and his followers have shown themselves in just the opposite light. Of their actions, Burke argues, there "is nothing simple, nothing manly, nothing ingenuous, open, decisive, or steady in the proceeding, with regard little to the continuance or the repeal of the taxes." Instead, Burke charges, their whole manner of proceeding "has an air of bitterness and fraud."

The preliminary work now set in place, Burke moves to consider the repeal's greater historical implications. His review will take shape in four phases, from the early Navigation Act of 1660 to Grenville's policy, from there to Rockingham's first ministry, to the Revenue Act of 1767. This narrative occupies most of the *Taxation* and facilitates most of its rhetorical gestures. More detailed than even the preceding review, it is offered, Burke promises, "not for the sake of telling you a long story . . . but for the sake of the weighty instruction that, I flatter myself, will necessary result from it." The narrative does in fact provide for this didactic purpose, but its rhetorical force can be accounted for on other grounds. Burke hopes to convince his audience that the recent legislation on America has departed dramatically from a proven course of advantage. Not at all coincidentally, that course, Burke would have his audience believe, was last tried by the Rockingham administration of 1765–66. In this way, the long narrative serves the dual purpose of giving historical sweep to Burke's argument and of allowing him to locate his players in his story. The narrative proper will henceforth be punctuated by character descriptions, and together these synchronic and diachronic depictions will advance Burke's rhetorical aim.

Burke's story begins in the halcyon years before 1764, when colonial policy was "purely commercial" and, thus, not designed for revenue production. As such, it was monopolistic, Burke admits, but the advantages to both England and the colonies were then remarkable. In words presaging his famous passage in the *Speech on Conciliation* a year later, Burke dwells on the wisdom of that ancient policy. Because it was no strange innovation—indeed, it had grown up with the colonies themselves—the system of commercial monopoly was never seriously questioned. And, Burke insists, it worked. "Nothing in the history of mankind is like their [the colonies'] progress," Burke says, and proceeds to create an image of a lost golden age. It is an image Burke will return to more than once as he dramatizes England's fall from grace: "For my part, I never cast an eye on their flourishing commerce and their cultivated and commodious life, but they seem to me rather an ancient nation grown to perfection through a long series of fortunate events and a trade of successful industry, accumulating wealth in many centuries, than a set of miserable outcasts, a few years ago, not as much sent as thrown out, on the bleak and barren shore of a desolate wilderness, 3,000 miles from all socialized intercourse." Here Burke couples wonder and pathos, and the result is a composite picture of America as being at once beautified and wretched. The intrusion of measures for revenue, together with monopoly, is accordingly nothing but "an unnatural union—perfect, uncompensated slavery."

Portrait 1: Grenville

At this point in the narrative Burke makes a transition into the second phase of his review. This phase is marked by the first of his character portraits and so interrupts the narrative progression. Burke's reflection on the recently deceased Grenville is notable for its lack of rancor and self-conscience effort at restraint. At the same time, Burke exploits the occasion not only to reflect on Grenville's complicity in the Stamp Act and the harmful consequences attending it, but also to dwell at some length on Grenville's quality of mind. The sketch itself represents an abrupt shift in tone, and for a time the reader is relieved of historical detail. Burke's portrait, moreover, asks the reader to see in a different way than the proceeding argument. Slowing down the pace of the speech, Burke presents a study in character quite distinct from the inferential rigor of his narrative. Here the reader is more a spectator, involved as a reader but welcomed into the reflective mood of the speaker. The general impression is striking; Burke induces the reader to join him in an epideictic gaze on rhetorical character. Neither laudatory nor overtly critical, Burke's composition is instead designed as a eulogy on both Grenville and his politics. Part lament and part instruction, the set piece allows Burke to account for political crises in the human terms of individual character.

Although Burke is careful to respect Grenville's memory, he has no doubt as to the late ministry's culpability. The new colonial policy of revenue generation was Grenville's, and while perhaps well intentioned, the system was deeply flawed. Such are the expected results, Burke explains, when political affairs are shaped by limited perspective. In words that echo and carry forward his earlier discussion on the importance of "large and liberal ideas in the management of great affairs," Burke traces Grenville's folly to his quality of mind. Grenville understood the detail, Burke says, but "he did not seem to have his view, at least equally, carried to the total circuit of our affairs. He generally considered his objects in light that were rather too detached."

As Burke proceeds to elaborate on Grenville's character, all discussion of the immediate political issues ceases. The change in direction arrests the forward motion of the narrative, and Burke can now recover the psychological sources of Grenville's politics. He thus individuates ministerial policy by embodying it, and he performs a kind of political autopsy on Grenville and his legacy. Grenville was, Burke insists, a "first-rate figure in this country. With a masculine understanding of a stout and resolute heart, he had an application undissipated and unwearied." The early strokes of Burke's description continue in this positive fashion and give to the portrait a sense of balance and objectivity. Even as he admits to Grenville's ambition, Burke is careful to qualify the criticism. "If he was ambitious, I will say this for him, his ambition was of a noble and generous strain." In lines that recall Burke's earlier attack in *Discontents*, the paragraph concludes by praising Grenville outright: "It was to raise himself, not by the low, pimping politics of a court, but to win his way to power through the labourious gradations of public service, and to secure to himself a well-earned rank in Parliament by a thorough knowledge of its constitution and perfect practice on all its business."

All this is, in effect, a gesture of friendship, offered to both Grenville and the audience as a sign of the speaker's judicious intentions. By identifying Grenville as the source of conflict with the colonies, the speaker grounds his changes in human agency; this grounding in turn serves as a foundation upon which Burke can extend his deliberation on political character. It is important that Burke's indictment is not limited to Grenville alone; he is, by direct implication, condemning the political judgment of all those who share Grenville's attributes of character. The portrait is in this sense a case study in political blindness, meant to apply whenever similar action can be found. By 1774, the audience need not look far to get the point.

The great lesson of Grenville's policy is that events had outstripped the Ministry's capacity to cope with them. Grenville lacked perspective, Burke reminds the reader again, and this "habit" could be traced to his professional training. Burke admits to thinking the law "one of the first and noblest of human sciences." But as a profession, it fails "to open and to liberalize the mind." As Grenville moved from the practice of law into office, these habits of mind remained characteristic; indeed, his very competence in the former threatened his talents for the latter. Burke thinks it a general principle "that men too much conversant in office are rarely minds of remarkable enlargement." This limited competence is suitable for public affairs when all is settled and the nation at peace. However, Burke warns, "when the high-roads are broken up, and the waters out, when a new and troubled scene is opened, and the file affords no precedent, then it is that a greater knowledge of mankind, and a far more extensive comprehension of things is requisite than ever office gave or than office can ever give."

When political circumstances became heated, Grenville lacked the political character to respond appropriately. Burke's portrait masks what is in effect an ad hominem attack on Grenville and his policies; and although it is expressed in relatively benign terms, it undermines confidence in the late leader, his legacy, and those who are now revealed to think as he thought. Burke is setting up the first in a series of object lessons in political judgment, and he will use this particular instance as a negative reflection of one to follow. The legalistic and overly constrained perspective of Grenville, this pinched and illiberal mind, will stand in explicit contrast to Burke's beloved Rockingham ministry.

Over and against the disastrous policy of the Grenville ministry, Burke poses the first Rockingham administration. The contrast is drawn as much by distinctions of character as by specific policy, and it sets in motion Burke's return to historical narrative. As the argument takes this turn, we note a dramatic change in the story itself; as if infused by the vigor of the subject, the account of Rockingham's repeal of the Stamp Act is charged with rhetorical energy. Here we see the first of many moments in the speech when the portraits are displayed as objects of moral deliberation and as a means to reinvigorate the narrative.

Portrait 2: Rockingham

In one of Burke's few autobiographical references, he initiates the portrait by dwelling on his own role in recent affairs. It was, he assures the audience, a very minor one indeed. But such anonymity, Burke argues, is precisely why his account should be trusted. The passage functions to introduce Rockingham dramatically, casting Burke's obscurity against the nobleman's great generosity of spirit. "In the year 1765," Burke begins, "being in a very private station, far enough from any line of business, than having the honor of a seat in this House, it was my fortune, unknowing and unknown to the then ministry . . . to become connected with a very noble person, and at the head of the Treasury department." In spite of his relatively minor station, Burke was able to perceive in Rockingham qualities of mind and character virtuous enough to command his enduring loyalty: "I did see in that noble person such sound principles, such an enlargement of mind, such clear and rigorous sense and such unshakable fortitude, as have bound me, as well as others much better than me, by an inviolable attachment to him from that time forward."

The implied contrast with Grenville is played out in the ensuing passages, where Burke details efforts to repeal the Stamp Act. As the narrative picks up again, the reader becomes aware of a quickened pace, and without reading too much into the speech, we can perceive its substance reflected in its tone. Burke's admiration of Rockingham becomes a celebration of political virtue, the description a litany of heroic traits. Confronted by opposition to repeal, Rockingham was "not afraid steadily to look in the face that glaring and dazzling influence at which the eyes of eagles have blanched." In contrast to his preceding charges of ministerial waffling, Rockingham's conduct is described as resolute and principled; in short, his political virtue proved equal to the circumstances. Whereas Grenville was unable to embrace the whole and its particulars and was unable to fix an advantageous line of conduct, Rockingham stood steady. "There were in both Houses," Burke recalls, "new and menacing appearances that might very naturally drive any other than a most resolute minister from his measure or from his station."

As Burke's description of the repeal thickens in detail, the emergent image takes the shape of an idealized representation of political virtue. It is, moreover, virtue in action, virtue revealed and affirmed within the shifting demands of politics. Rockingham is made to stand out and against his opposition; thus positioned, Burke attributes to him near mythic qualities of political rectitude. The struggle, indeed, becomes in Burke's language an epic confrontation: "Earth below shook, heaven above menaced; all the elements of ministerial safety were dissolved. It was in the midst of this chaos of plots and counterplots, it was in the midst of this complicated warfare against public opposition and private treachery, that the firmness of that noble person was put to the proof. He never stirred from his ground—no, not an inch. He remained fixed and determined in principle, in measure, and in conduct. He practiced no managements. He secured no retreat. He sought no apology." Few among the opposition would doubt that Burke's depiction was, to say the very least, glorified. But like his portrait of Grenville, its rhetorical appeal is not so much mimetic accuracy as dramatic characterization. Here again, individual character embodies the political virtues Burke celebrates; he can then give to these virtues an animated and enduring presence. The image is designed accordingly to enlarge audience perception, to create a community of sentiment grateful for the chance to share in Rockingham's glory.

Burke's key rhetorical gesture, therefore, is to induce his audience to assume the same "enlarged mentality," to appreciate the "large and liberal ideas in the management of great affairs" he spoke of in the introduction. And to command this perspective, Burke implies, is to see virtue as it is exercised individually and historically. The repeal of the Stamp Act was just such a moment, when the particular virtue of its key players created a collective sense of unified public action. "I declare for one," Burke says, "I never came with so much spirit into this House. It was a time for a *man* to act in. We had powerful enemies; but we had faithful and determined friends, and a glorious cause. We had a great battle to fight. . . . we did fight that day and conquer." The first two character portraits thus represent for Burke and his desired audience a clash in political virtues. Rhetorically, his depictions dramatize the contrast by highlighting modes of procedure and judgment. For Burke to make those portraits believable, he must give his audience a reason to believe; he offers an opportunity to repeat the glorious repeal of the Stamp Act by repealing the equally ignominious tea tax.

Burke's glorious recollection, like the Rockingham ministry itself, does not last long. Driven to defend the repeal from charges that it incited colonial rebellion, the speaker returns to his historical narrative. This interplay between reflections on character and detailed review is by now a dominant pattern in the speech, and it leads the reader to expect more of the same. Burke will in fact return shortly to another portrait, that of Lord Chatham, in what will become the most famous passage of the oration. For now, Burke must refute attacks on the repeal of the Stamp Act and on its implied principle of leniency. Encouraging his audience to assume a broad historical perspective, Burke promises to "clearly lay before you the state of America antecedently to that repeal, after the repeal, and since the renewal of the schemes of American taxation."

The following account plunges the reader back into the particulars of Anglo-American relations, and with characteristic vigor, Burke marshalls an array of proofs to vindicate the repeal. It is an agile performance, replete with letters and witnesses, attack and defense. For the reader, narrative and argument become indistinguishable; the ostensibly objective nature of the account provides veracity to Burke's refutation. As the review concludes, Burke confidently declares that far from the cause of colonial dissent, the repeal was in truth the very embodiment of political wisdom. The objective force of the narrative and the refutation lead Burke to conclude: "I am bold to say that so sudden and calm recovered after violent a storm is without parallel in history. . . . after this experience, nobody shall persuade me, when a whole people are concerned, that acts of levity are not means of conciliation."

Portrait 3: Lord Chatham

Passing now into the third phase of the oration, Burke presents to his audience the formidable figure of Lord Chatham. This characterization is justly thought a masterwork of political depiction. But aside from its sardonic humor, the passage functions rhetorically as an elaborate argumentum ad hominem. Burke has already delivered seemingly judicious portraits, and he is likewise here careful to balance the negative with positive description. The space between Chatham's character and his legacy is so great, however, and the contrast with Rockingham so pronounced, that the entire passage becomes devastatingly ironic. Burke, it would seem, trusts his audience to appreciate that irony; and to the extent that they together recognize Chatham's ambivalent legacy, they come to expose together the deep failings of his political character.

That Burke had personal reasons to suspect Chatham's career is of course suppressed. Chatham followed fast on the dissolution of Rockingham's ministry and had since been anything but a reliable ally in opposition. Burke is anxious, therefore, to assume a posture of proper respect, a stance familiar as the deference paid to those no longer significant as political actors. Quoting Lucien, Burke celebrates Chatham as "claram et venerabile Nomen/Gentibus, et multum nostrae quod proderat urbi—An illustrious name, venerable to the world, and one which has much helped our city." As we might expect, however, Burke's is no ceremonial speech, and he designs his digressions for specific ends. He is chiefly concerned to explain the failure of post-Rockingham ministries, and he will not allow his audience to dwell for too long on Chatham's ostensible virtues.

The opening lines of the passage work to ensure that his audience not be marked by Chatham's legacy, a legacy long in competition with Rockingham's. Nevertheless, Burke says, "the venerable age of this great man, his merited rank, his superior eloquence, his splendid qualities, his eminent service, the vast space he fills in the eye of mankind, and more than all the rest, his fall from power, which like death, canonizes and sanctifies a great character, will not suffer me to censure any part of his conduct." Burke's due is quickly paid, however, and the following line initiates an extended attack on Chatham's judgment and ministerial command. Unlike Grenville, who suffered from an inability to see general principles at work in particular events and problems, Chatham is here made to suffer from the opposite malady. "For a wise man," Burke says, Chatham "seemed to me at that time to be governed too much by general maxims." The most regretful of these, Burke implies, was the cant phrase "not men but measures." That Chathamite maxim proved his undoing, as it failed to produce a coherent political program or ministry. Because the depiction itself has become a classic of rhetorical depiction, it is best quoted at length:

He made an administration so checkered and speckled, he put together a piece of joinery so crossly indented and whimsically dovetailed, a cabinet so variously inlaid, such a piece of diversified mosaic, such a tessellated pavement without cement—here a bit of black stone and there a bit of white, patriots and courtiers, king's friends and republicans, Whigs and Tories, treacherous friends and open enemies—that it was, indeed, a very curious show, but utterly unsafe to touch and unsure to stand on. The colleagues whom he had assorted stared at each other, and were obliged to ask—"Sir, your name?"—"Sir, you have the advantage of me."—"Mr. Such-a-one."— "I beg a thousand pardons."—I venture to say, it did so happen that persons had a single office divided between them, who had never spoke to each other in their lives, until they found themselves, they knew not how, pigging together, heads and points, in the same truckle bed.

Here is an exquisite bit of mock-epideictic. With the very pace and structure of its clauses, the passage mimics Chatham's allegedly disordered or overly wrought ministry. The purported virtues of coalition government, at least on the scale represented here, are strategically reversed; acting "too much on general maxims," Chatham had created a virtual parody of his own political principles. Burke, of course, is having fun with the humorless Chatham, but he is quick to impress upon his audience how serious the consequences of such policies could be. Circumstance, as always with Burke, give the lie to principle, and consequences to judgment. Chatham, Burke invites us to believe, had been exposed by both.

If we recall Burke's defense of party as a form of concerted action, we can see how far Chatham's ministry had drifted from Burke's standard. In *Discontents* Burke had insisted that party gave direction and effect to deliberation. Chatham, having renounced party as unnatural and dangerous, thus invited his own ruin. So great was the confusion marking Chatham's ministry, Burke recalls, "that his own principles could not possibly have any effect or influence in the conduct of affairs. If he ever fell into a fit of the gout, or if any other cause withdraw him from public cases, principles directly the contrary were sure to predominate."

At this late stage in Burke's oration, the lesson has begun to take on a familiar air. The speaker here again works through a series of graphic contrasts the better to dramatize his standards of political virtue. If he has been at all successful, Burke will have habituated his audience to see in Chatham an exemplar of poor judgment. Like Grenville before him, Chatham suffered from lack of vision, and his personal instability was but a reflection of the politics he created. In the end Chatham's legacy is pronounced a sorry combination of irony and pathos. In words that forecast a dominant theme in the Bristol address, Burke describes the consequences of Chatham's enigmatic leadership: "Deprived of his guiding influence," Burke explains, "the sundry ministries were whirled about, the sport of every gust, and easily driven into any port." Worse, the disorder opened an opportunity for those who would make a mockery of Chatham's high-minded principles: "as those who joined with them in manning the vessels were the most directly opposite to his opinions, measures, and character, and far the most artful and most powerful of the set, they easily prevailed, so as to seize upon the vacant, unoccupied, and derelict minds of his friends; and instantly they turned the vessel wholly out of the course of his policy." Chaotic, vulnerable, ostensibly strong but essentially weak; as Burke describes Chatham, so he implicates his political virtue.

Portrait 4: Townshend

If Chatham's folly was to misconstrue the nature of leadership, Townshend's was to lack the capacity for leadership whatsoever. Burke accordingly portrays Townshend's role in Anglo-American affairs in a striking composition of rapid strokes. Balancing his genuine fondness against regret for Townshend's shortcomings, Burke moves toward his conclusion with a lingering retrospective on politics and character. It is, the notorious sketch of Chatham notwithstanding, the finest of Burke's renditions. And as the final portrait of the oration, it embraces many of the features and nuances of those preceding it: quality of statecraft, capacity for judgment, virtue of character, and character of virtue. Burke thus leads his audience to see in Townshend's career a cautionary tale on the limits of personality as a substitute for character. Chatham was too strong, too strange and independent; Townshend, conversely, was too eager to please. Either way, Burke implies, politics suffers.

To Burke, Townshend was "the delight and ornament of this House, and the charm of every private society which he honored with his presence." The speaker seems genuinely devoted to Townshend's memory, and he can trust his audience to put aside partisan interests for the moment as they jointly reflect on the late minister. Like all his compositions, this one is complex, especially so, and we now expect another side of Townshend's character to be revealed. Still, Burke works cautiously. He is especially impressed by Townshend's deliberative talents: "He stated his matter skillfully and powerfully. He particularly excelled in a most luminous explanation and display of his subject. His style of argument was neither trite and vulgar nor subtle and abstruse. He hit the House just between wind and water." Such talents, Burke reminds his audience, come at a cost, and the price paid by Townshend proved his undoing. The minister, Burke concludes the paragraph, "conformed exactly to the temper of the House, and he seemed to guide, because he was also sure to follow it."

For the first and only time in the oration Burke comments on his strategic digression. The intervention at first appears to break up the portrait, to interrupt the process of creation with which we are becoming familiar. In effect, however, it elevates the commentary above the merely personal, allowing the speaker to control the aim and effect of his argument. It is, in short, as much reflection on his own mode of deliberation as on Townshend's and that of the House. This reflection, in turn, positions speaker, audience, and argument within a more general complex of political and moral action. "In the eventful history of the revolution of America," Burke explains, "the characters of such men are of much importance. Great men are the guideposts and land-marks of the state." Burke's insistence on the centrality of the individual to the conduct of affairs is resolute; character is the source of all action, and ultimately its only rationale. "The credit of such men at court, or in the nation, is the sole cause of all the public measures," Burke says, and reminds his audience that the "subject is instructive to those who wish to form themselves on whatever excellence has gone before them." Inevitably, their excellence is depicted as excellence of character revealed in the deliberative process. By demonstrating that excellence through and in the speech itself, Burke can hope to be the object of his own instruction.

Townshend's ill-advised Revenue Act of 1767 represents the fourth and final phase of Burke's narrative. It was, he argues, the bad issue of both its author and the House, the expected consequence of poor judgment. In this case, at least, the cause could be traced to the character of both. By passing the Stamp Act in 1765, repealing it a year later, and reintroducing Townshend's duties afterwards, the House had shown itself, if nothing else, not inclined toward obstinacy. The problem, Burke reasons, is that Parliament had failed to perceive in obstinacy a set of attending virtues. Burke had castigated Grenville for being too rigid, for lacking perspective and the freedom that enlarged vision grants. Townshend, like the body he represented, had proven vulnerable to precisely the opposite. Just as Grenville had undermined his political virtue by being too obstinate, Commons had undermined itself by not being obstinate enough. As it happens, Burke explains, "Almost the whole line of the great and masculine virtues, constancy, gravity, magnanimity, fortitude, fidelity, and firmness" are variations on obstinance. Unfortunately, Townshend's own waffling judgment and irresolute ways mirrored perfectly the personality of the House. Confronted with the need to tax the Americans, conciliate them, and placate merchant interests simultaneously, Ministry and House spun an exquisite but weak web of policy. "This fine-spun scheme," Burke notes, "had the usual fate of all exquisite policy. But [Townshend's] original plan of the duties, and the mode of executing that plan, both arose singly and solely from a love of our applause. He was truly the child of the House. He never thought, he never did, or said anything, but with a view to you. He every day adapted himself to your disposition, and adjusted himself before it as at a looking-glass."

Conclusion

Burke's peroration, like that of *Discontents*, culminates the values and imperatives developed through the argument. Here they are given forceful expression as both warning and exhortation. Moreover, Burke draws on the preceding arguments to strengthen his more general concerns for the integrity of political action. A policy of leniency and concession, Burke promises his audience, means that "when you have recovered your old, your strong, your tenable position, . . . approve the ancient policy and practice of the empire as a rampart against the speculations of innovators on both sides of the questions, you will stand on great, manly, and sure ground. On this solid basis fix your machines, and they will draw worlds toward you."

As the speech moves toward closure, its final passages reiterate and strengthen this image of fixed principle. It has been the touchstone of each of Burke's portraits, and it gives to his plea for levity the force of moral character—his own, that of his argument, and ultimately that of his audience. Posing past folly against future good, the speaker assures the House that it is capable of right reason and that its exercise is strong enough to withstand the tempest into which the nation had been thrown. Burke reveals the advantages of acting thus, and so provides an incentive and reward for returning a Rockinghamite policy. But more than this, Burke offers a vision of sorts and asks that his audience, in going backward, join him in looking ahead. There, in an uncertain future, Burke cannot guarantee that lenience "would cause Americans' passion to subside, or the reverse would increase its folly." All that, he admits, is "in the hand of Providence." But as a principle of right action, Burke implies, "I should confide in the prevailing virtue and efficacious operation of leniency, though working in darkness and in chaos, in the midst of all this unnatural and turbid combination, I should hope it might produce order in beauty in the end."

In the event, the bill was defeated 182 to 49. This too was to become a pattern of Burke's life in opposition. Its meaning and force cannot, however, be restricted to such standards of effect—at least, not if we are to engage the speech on the level it deserves. In Burke's final words, rather, we can capture its enduring value. "Order in beauty": as a description of Burke's rhetorical portraiture, these words signify at once the ideological content of the address and its formal ingenuity. Like all powerful discourses, it gives the audience reason to believe. In this case, however, the modes of inducement are not so much inferential as affective. Put another way, Burke so structures his argument as to invite his auditor to see in the portraits the virtual embodiment of virtue—and its opposite. Acquiescing to Burke's argument is not then sheerly a matter of assent to its logic; for the speech to work, Burke must teach his listeners and reader how to see, and in seeing, to understand. Hence the formulation of these portraits as hermeneutic keys; they provide the means, incentive, and reward for the audience to see as the speaker sees.

Finally, Burke's strategic recourse to epideictic convention serves his purposes well. As the ancient rhetorical art of praise and blame, epideictic oratory is particularly suited to studies of character, especially as character is disclosed within the terms and images of public life. Burke's epideictic allows us to seize the narrative march of events, to stall it long enough to recognize the hands of human agency, and so to isolate the motive forces of political action. In this world and by this way of telling, Burke understood, virtue was best revealed before the eyes of human community.

3

Enacting Rhetorical Judgment in the *Speech on Conciliation*

As is commonly the fate of Edmund Burke's art, the legacy of his *Speech on Conciliation* remains unfixed. Historians and critics unfailingly applaud the speech as a hallmark in the tradition of Western oratory, in turn pointing to its wealth of imagery, political insight, and humanity. But aside from this uniform appreciation of its aesthetic qualities, consensus stops short of investing Burke's masterpiece with historical or conceptual significance. This disjunction between rhetorical and political judgment finds its voice, ironically, in the appraisal of Burke's friend and patron, Lord Rockingham. The Marquis, upon hearing Burke's address of 22 March 1775, wrote, "I never felt a more complete satisfaction on hearing any speech, than I did on yours this day; the matter and the manner were equally perfect, and in spite of envy and malice and in spite of all politics, I will venture to prognosticate that there will be but one opinion, in regard to the wonderful ability of the performance."[1] Rockingham, as it turns out, was quite right; "in spite of all politics," Burke's speech has been ever since deemed an exemplary performance. But can Burke's masterpiece ever be taken seriously as anything more than a performance?

Then as now, Burke's oration has been received with an ambivalence typical of his legacy in general. The standard of effect continues to vex our understanding of Burke's achievement, and we may attribute this evaluation at least in part to the verdicts of modern scholarship. Historians of a generation ago were inclined to judge the speech most harshly; while conceding it artistic achievement, they consistently have relegated the speech to the backwaters of hopeless causes and misplaced idealism. Ritcheson's study of Anglo-American politics during the age of colonial conflict, for instance, concludes: "looking nostalgically to the past, Burke sought once more to ignore the ugly question of right, a question which, once raised, had made a return to the old system as impossible as a return to childhood."[2] Whether in fact Burke was guilty of such political nostalgia is certainly arguable; in any case, Ritcheson's assessment is not isolated. Watson's analysis of the reign of George III sounds the theme again by lamenting that "Burke had, in the mysterious alchemy of his mind, turned this practical compromise into a great living principle of a commonwealth. He had done so, however, for the admiration of posterity and not for use in 1775."[3] Even those traditionally more inclined to sympathize with Burke's idealism stress its futility and desperation. Guttridge is willing to grant that Burke's appeal is "a noble one." But the argument was also "extremely convenient; for the Whigs had nothing to suggest except to appeal to Time the healer, and to leave the future to take care of itself."[4] More recent studies of Burke and his times are more sensitive to Burke's motives, but few would regard the speech as a success in any meaningful sense of the word.[5]

The joint themes of futility and impracticality running throughout these observations are telling. Most important, they presume a certain teleology and judge the speech according to its failure to achieve its alleged ends. The assumption is misleading, and it badly stands in need of reexamination in the light of historical, biographical, and textual evidence. Such evidence, we find, supports an entirely different understanding of the speech. Far more than a hopeless but elegant appeal for imperial concord, the *Speech on Conciliation* is a declaration and demonstration of Whig ideology in its moment of crisis. I shall argue here that Burke's speech may be understood in a more general sense as an act of exemplary judgment. Its significance, accordingly, lies neither in its literary qualities nor in its expediency (or lack thereof). Rather, as an act of judgment, the oration instantiates Burke's directives on political virtue. The rationale and advantages of so approaching the speech may be indicated in a review of its aims, historical background, and textual conventions.

Confronted with the fact of the proposal's overwhelming defeat, sympathetic students of Burke have located his achievement in the more rarefied realms of history, philosophy, and aesthetic appeal. There is much in the *Speech on Conciliation* that lends itself to this kind of analysis, but its immediate aims and context cannot be simply wished away. At its most elemental level, the speech was delivered to secure Parliament's consent for Burke's conciliatory measures. It failed to do so, 70 to 278. Judged against a simple standard of effect, the speech must be regarded as a failure. Although Burke's oration may have been hopelessly idealistic, so the lore reads, it was nevertheless a masterpiece of political reasoning and principle. In their effort to secure Burke's oration within the canon, his admirers seem to have lost sight of its character as a public, pragmatic act. It will therefore be useful to focus upon the speech within its immediate context as a preface to formal analysis.

As a constant presence in the House debates on the colonies, Burke understood clearly the sentiments of Commons and the chances for appeasement. Parliament was growing increasingly impatient with the refusal of the Americans to yield, and the Crown itself seemed intent upon breaking their rebellious spirit. Given this knowledge, Burke offered his plan of conciliation as much to display the principles of his party as to capture votes. But to do this he had to articulate those principles in the concrete terms of political deliberation. To do otherwise, in fact, would run counter to the very standards of utility and judgment which the speech announces and acts upon. Within a context of party ideology and a perceived threat to Whig principles, the speech may be seen as a composite of deliberative and epideictic conventions. As a celebration of Whig principle, the speech glories in a past sanctioned morally by human nature and the consent of the political community. But in order to reclaim that past, Burke not only had to ground party ideology in history, but also had to expose Lord North's program as essentially ahistorical—that is, without precedent and hence without moral sanction. How Burke achieves this result constitutes the rhetorical action and success of the oration. Driving a wedge between his party and North's administration, Burke locates the proper exercise of political judgment in a stratum between abstract issues of right and particular questions of expediency. He exposes, conversely, the policy of the administration as the product of poor judgment: overly rationalistic, detached, abstract, impractical. In this sense, Burke's *Speech on Conciliation* may be deemed a success—not in terms of final divisions, but as a political statement on the proper grounds of political judgment.

At the same time, Burke's oration speaks to an audience more distanced than the actors of 1775. Burke was a political thinker, and his principles were meant to extend beyond the immediate audiences and questions of the moment.[6] Although he was not a philosopher, he nevertheless explored the nature of politics at a level higher than most, and he typically treated problems of the state within the conventional forms of public discourse. At this level, his audience expands to include those outside of Parliament and, indeed, generations not yet born. In Burke's oration, as in most of his other rhetoric, there are accordingly two audiences being addressed: an audience situated within an immediate spatial and temporal relationship; and a historical audience of ideal listeners, able by virtue of its distance to judge with accuracy and insight. The respective appeals are not, however, in contest or inconsistent. In keeping with his general position—that the principles of his party represent a model of proper political action—Burke displays to both audiences the virtues of practical reason and prudence of action. These principles are in turn established on the basis of experience and utility; that is, they are not abstract axioms or mere platitudes of statecraft. In speaking to both audiences, Burke seeks to provide a rationale for action grounded in principle and expedience: principle as it is generated from historical perspective, expedience as a question of propriety. So understood, this rationale offers to his audiences an exemplary standard of judgment. And in this way, Burke's oration is, in fact, a repudiation of his parliamentary audience—but only in the sense that he confronts its momentary failure to exercise proper judgment. Burke appeals rather to the values and expectations of the audience in a different time, a moment in the past when it understood better than now the principles of right reason and action. Burke had, therefore, to reconfigure the historical understanding of his audience to satisfy his "obligations to party and principle."

Within this historical and political context, we are in a position to understand Burke's *Speech on Conciliation* in a new light. The speech is not simply solicitous, and as such doomed to failure, but advisory as well. By all accounts the Rockingham Whigs were in a perilous state of disarray and ennui. Burke's oration was thus remedial and justificatory; it was in fact a performance, but a performance meant to illustrate the virtues of its own argument. Burke was seeking to resurrect an ideology failing badly, even as he announced and acted upon its avowed principles. The rhetorical action of the speech is therefore exemplary; and Burke, by repeatedly grounding these principles in particular historical circumstances, provides a vision of what his party may become. Both the referent of the speech and its controlling animus concern action. Hence the speech works to create a particular kind of perspective, and it relies upon the willingness of the audience to recognize in present circumstances reconfigurations of the past. Here is the basis of judgment and the rationale for action Burke would have his audience understand; and to the extent that it does understand, the audience reaffirms its commitment to the Whig past and its legacy. Burke, in short, speaks in order to make present the meaning of the past; to speak in this situation is therefore itself exemplary, an act that cannot be judged on the basis of mere House divisions.

A careful reading of the structural and imagistic movements that control the speech bears out this alternative perspective. The formal unity of Burke's oration is established on two levels, each reflecting the speaker's concern for the proper relationship between order and action. At one level, the speech is patterned on models of classical oratory; it thereby manifests an established order and its arguments are rationalized by relatively abstract considerations of form. At another level, however, the speech unfolds without clear divisions and without the aid of orthodox principles of structure. Here meaning is generated on the basis of certain psychological forces, made evident in the evolution of its structure and appeals. In this sense the speech may be understood as an instantiation of Burke's principle of judgment. For Burke, proper judgment involves the right ordering of rational principles and emotional warrants to action. He who would sustain a balance between these motive forces is the ideal practical politician, allowing neither sheer rationalism nor simple emotions to determine the course of political action. Hence the structures of the speech support Burke's ends: by showing himself to be rational he endorses the role of principle in proper judgment; and by appealing to the emotionally grounded patriotism of his audience, he complements rationalism with the power of experience and collective history. Insofar as this relationship is revealed structurally, it sustains the development of the speech throughout.

The familiarity of this structure should not, however, deflect attention from another equally important source of meaning. Burke seeks to induce a perspective ordered by experience, a perspective that is located in history, not outside of it. The essential action of the text cannot therefore be fully explained by the divisions and categories identified above, if only because they abstract from the particular requirements and motives of the occasion. In a very basic sense, the movement of Burke's oration cannot be apprehended within classical forms. As it moves toward its end in action, the speech reflects an ever-widening perspective directing that action. This perspective is made possible by an accretion of detail and principle working interdependently to form the basis of proper judgment. Thus the enormous amount of detail that Burke provides is more than evidentiary support; conventionally understood, it represents as well a commitment to the particulars of political action. At the same time, the many axioms that characterize Burke's political perspective indicate his capacity for reasoning from principle. Together, the interplay of particular and principle directs the progress of the speech. As he moves through the speech, Burke employs this capacity for practical reason to order the particulars of historical experience into a rationale for action. The more his audience recognizes this history, the greater its perspective becomes, and the greater its capacity for right action. Burke must then present this history in all its variety, and yet order it as a form of moral sanction. In this context the action of the speech is cumulative, building principle upon fact and recognizing in fact the utility of principle.

More specifically, the progression of the text is directed through three phases: an ostensibly objective review of America and the facts of her condition; an argument for restoring colonial loyalty through self-taxation; and a defense of the resolutions as the best course of future action. The oration advances in this way from time past through the present to time future. Each phase in turn demonstrates the proper constituents of political action, moving from fact (narration) to principle (argument) and culminating in action (resolutions). The meaning of the speech cannot then be structured within the classical form of the oration only; it must, in addition, be identified as it progresses through these temporal and conceptual phases.

But the key to understanding the movement of the text is to see in these phases the repeated and relentless accommodation of immediate problems into a greater historical perspective. This relationship between the constraints of the moment and the prospects of historical understanding orders the separation of Burke and North. As the oration progresses, the accretion of examples works to identify Burke and his party with history itself and to expose North and his administration as being blind to its directives. The elemental action of the text is therefore a process of identification and division; it is a movement repeated throughout the oration in different contexts and different phases. But the lesson Burke would have his audience understand remains the same: right action is a function of practical reason, itself the result of historically grounded judgment.

The rhetorical form of the oration served Burke's purposes well. It had long been employed by opposition members as a means to challenge, with relative freedom, the policies of those in power and had developed certain generic traits of character and idiom. As an oral practice, the oration allowed for a degree of spontaneity not so easily produced in the political essay. Its adaptability to the moment, however, often meant that its effect was fleeting, especially in an era of limited parliamentary reporting. As a result, those who wished to have their sentiments recorded were compelled to print speeches in pamphlet form and have them distributed by area booksellers. The *Speech on Conciliation* was offered in this way to a greater and more distant public than could be found within Commons. Such a practice also helps to explain the speech's elevated tone and philosophic appeal. In Burke's hands the oration represents an ideal rhetorical form, insofar as it is fixed by historical convention and is, at the same time, a response to immediate public issues. The form of the oration thus instantiates the very play of fixity and flux that shapes the *Speech on Conciliation*.

Introduction

The *ingratio* that initiates the speech and provides conventional access into the argument is at first review unsurprising. As one of "many examples in the speech of humility assumed for the sake of oratorical effect," this facet of Burke's oration is typically ignored.[7] If commented upon at all, it is seen as simply fulfilling a generic expectation. There is some loss, however, in hurrying over the *ingratio*, for here we find a précis of the speech as a whole. What appears to be a passing reference to the past, for example, can be taken as a telling account of circumstances leading up to the speech; and what may pass for affected humility is an ironic assertion of character. This alignment of character and circumstances defines the rhetorical movement of the *ingratio* and so anticipates the tensive quality of the entire speech. In particular, Burke intimates what will become the major claim in this battle between the ancients and the moderns, the fixity which historical perspective brings to the flux of experience.

Burke's avowed surprise at the return of North's bill is tempered by a religious sensibility that sees in it an "omen," a "providential favor," possibly a "superior warning voice." Whatever its source, the returned bill functions synecdochically in the speech, as a moment in which the past—seemingly lost—is recalled to the present. As such, it provides a renewed opportunity to act, and Burke says, "we are put once more in position of our deliberative capacity, upon a business so very questionable in its nature, so very uncertain in its issue." Against this uncertainty, Burke counsels attention to "the whole of it together; and to review the subject with an unusual degree of care and calmness."[8] Though brief, the first paragraph suggests an intense concern for temporal relationships and indicates the grounds of proper judgment at the moment when past meets present.

As Burke recounts his role in the repeal of the Stamp Tax nine years earlier, his character accrues the benefits of past action, and we begin to witness the beginning of a long process of character construction. Burke, newly elected to Commons, had then found himself "a partaker in a very high trust," and lacking natural talent, he was "obliged to take more than common pains" to instruct himself on American affairs. As a result of this self-education, Burke had developed some "fixed ideas concerning the general policy of the British Empire." "Something of this sort seemed to me indispensable," Burke concludes, "in order, amidst so vast a fluctuation of passion and opinions, to concentre my thoughts, to ballast my conduct, to preserve me from being blown about by every fashionable doctrine. I really did not think it safe or manly to have fresh principles to seek upon every fresh mail which should arrive from America." The nautical metaphor, a favorite resource of Burke's, here suggests a standard of judgment and action. Fixed by principle and steadied by his knowledge of American affairs, Burke was then able to act consistently and honorably while others yielded to the sirens of innovation and experiment. The metaphor, of course, has its literal reference, in that England and America are indeed separated by a vast and fluctuating ocean. It is a reality Burke exploits with great effect later in the speech. The aim now is to set the speaker's past action in relief to that of Parliament, and while Burke forbears from any direct indictment, the difference is clear enough. The following paragraphs thus recount the respective careers of Burke and of Commons since the repeal of the Stamp Tax.

The current state of affairs, we learn, is not the result of the Rockingham policy of conciliation, but of departing from that policy and from the principles that guided the administration generally. In contradistinction to the waffling and ineffective action of Commons, Burke says, "I have continued ever since, without the least deviation, in my original sentiments. Whether this be owing to an obstinate perseverance in error, or to a religious adherence to what appears to me truth and reason, it is iniquity to judge." In the years since repeal, Parliament had made "more frequent changes in their sentiments and their conduct than could be justified in a particular person." Parliament's failure, in short, was not in the past, but in its ability to sustain that past. And so, Burke concludes, "by a variety of experiments that important country has been brought to her present situation—a situation which I will not miscall, which I dare not name, which I scarcely know how to comprehend in the terms of any description."

Far from being a posture of humility, then, the *ingratio* coordinates circumstances and character in such a manner as to make the speaker a virtual embodiment of past virtue. The brief narration making up the first eight paragraphs unfolds to reveal the past as a rationale for action in the present, and even as the *ingratio* appears to diminish the achievements of the speaker, it dramatizes the need for his leadership. This posture works to identify the proposition not so much with its author as with forces more fixed and powerful than mere human agency. Burke's maneuver thus grants to Commons the opportunity to judge without embarrassment: "I persuaded myself that you would not reject a reasonable proposition, because it had nothing but reason to recommend it. On the other hand, being totally destitute of all shadow of influence, natural or adventitious, I was very sure that if my proposition were futile or dangerous, if it were weakly conceived or improperly timed, there was nothing exterior to it, of power to awe, dazzle, or delude you. You will see it just as it is, and you will treat it just as it deserves." Burke sets up a key relationship between objective fact and political judgment that informs the speech generally; he later indicts North for his inability to see in the American situation objective constraints on policy. At the same time, Burke attempts to demonstrate his own capacity to derive principles of political action from material circumstances.

Thesis

"The proposition is peace." Burke's thesis could not be more blunt. It follows no apparent transition and precedes a lengthy and complex series of negative clauses. Its rhetorical effect, however, is dramatic. Syntactically it mimics the oppositions Burke seeks to establish, which in turn become the structural principles of the speech. Action rooted in historical understanding is distinguished by its natural simplicity; conduct initiated without precedent, without historical understanding, is marked by an artificial complexity and confusion. Thus the following negative clauses become a bill of particulars against North's administration, and more generally against its very manner of reasoning. "The proposition is peace," Burke states, but not peace "through the medium of war; not peace to be hunted through the labyrinth of intricate and endless negotiations; not peace to arise out of universal discord fomented from principle in all parts of the empire; not peace to depend on the judicial determination of perplexing questions, or the peace marking the shadowy boundaries of a complex government." Rather, Burke says, "it is simple peace, sought in its natural course, and its ordinary haunts." As it is framed above by short, propositional statements, so the indictment is framed below. The false peace of North's plan is labyrinthine, intricate, endless, perplexing, shadowy, and complex; Burke's is simple, natural, and ordinary. Only a bill predicated on proven principles and historical perspective can return the past to the present, can, Burke concludes, restore the "former unsuspecting confidence of the colonies in the mother country."

As "simple" and "ordinary" as Burke's proposition avowedly may be, its appeal is grounded in principle. The maxims that begin the tenth paragraph indicate Burke's tendency to generalize from the particular, to exercise the principle, and thereby to add force to his arguments as he returns again to particular issues. This interplay between the general and the particular informs the action of the later narration, but for now it works to distance Burke's bill further from North's. "Refined policy," Burke claims, "ever has been the parent of confusion." He would substitute instead "plain good intention" and a "genuine simplicity of heart." But precisely because, by his own admission, there is "nothing at all new and captivating" in Burke's proposal, because it has "nothing of the splendor of the project" of North's, the proposition commands assent. Unlike his own, North's project depends upon a "mode that is altogether new,— one that is, indeed, wholly alien from all the ancient methods and forms of Parliament."

What those "ancient methods and forms of Parliament" are we come to understand as the speech progresses. As Burke undertakes and develops each phase, we see that he is not only appealing to history as a form of proof, but he is enacting it, that the speech is itself a moment in its own history. It is a lesson on how to read the past, and insofar as the audience benefits from the lesson, it assents to the argument.

Narration

Burke's review of the Americans is throughout detailed, systematic, and factual. But while he locates the problem in phenomenal reality, Burke is careful to avoid mere litigation. The narrative, rather, brings to light the meaning of material circumstances. Facts provide the basis for judgment, and judgment in turn orders the meaning of facts. The narrative thereby frames a constant interplay between concrete reality and its interpretation. As a result of this interplay, the narrative generates a habitual perspective in which the past is made proximic to the present. As such, the past is itself exemplary and is embodied in one who exercises its lessons.

Between the past and the present are forces that, if recognized, give presence to history. The impetus of the past is most evident in the imagery that dominates the narrative: fecundity, familial attractions, and the inevitable progression of events. In every case, the past is not simply an option. Whatever the judgment that attends it, the past unfailingly makes itself present. Such, for example, is the problem of America's burgeoning population. While the House of

Commons interminably debates policy for a government of two million people, the number grows at a formidable rate. In fact, Burke warns, "your children do not grow faster from infancy to manhood, than they spread from families to communities, and from villages to nations." Given this state of affairs, Burke is adamant to adjust our response to it. With a thinly disguised attack on North's bill, Burke argues that "no partial, narrow, contracted, pinched, occasional system will be at all suitable to such an object." The failure of North's policy has been exactly this, that it failed to act according to observable realities, failed to understand the history of its own problem. This being the case, the colonial problem became greater than the Ministry's ability to handle it. North's government lacked perspective, and unable to understand America's strength, had trifled with it. However, Burke concludes, "you could at no time do so without guilt; and be assured you will not be able to do it long with impunity."

Nowhere in the speech is this sense of historical perspective so dramatically portrayed as in Burke's account of colonial commerce. After a relatively detailed review of Anglo-American trade, Burke slows the pace of the narrative, reflects upon the immediate occasion, and directs a contemplative gaze toward America. "It is good for us to be here," Burke explains. "We stand where we have an immense view of what is, and what is past." This perspective has been required by the demands of the moment, but it reveals much: "Clouds, indeed, and darkness rest upon the future." The sublimity of the image intensifies as the passage develops; here it is notable for its temporal referent. Sublimity of experience is ultimately an expansion of one's capacity for experience, and it is this capacity Burke exercises as he surveys the Americans. To enhance that prospect, Burke takes his audience upon an unmistakably Virgilian journey.

Marveling at the rapidity of English commercial growth, Burke employs the figure of one Lord Bathurst, whose life would have framed this development. At its beginning, Burke notes Bathurst would have been old enough *"acta parentum jam legere, et quae sit poterit cognoscere virtus."* Though misquoted, the allusion is telling and portends a number of similar references. Burke sees in this particular scenario an opportunity to dramatize his general argument—that we must "study the example of the forefathers, to learn what virtue is." The Virgilian maxim thus directs our attention to the proximity of its moral claim and shows Burke excavating texts of venerable wisdom. Developing the conceit further, Burke asks us to suppose that "the angel of this auspicious youth [Bathurst]" to have "drawn up the curtain and unfolded the rising glories of his country, and, whilst he was gazing with admiration on the then commercial grandeur of England, the genius should point out to him a little speck, scarcely visible in the mass of national interest, a small seminal principle rather than a formal body, and should tell him,—'Young man, there is America.'" It would take "all the sanguine credulity of youth," Burke continues, for Bathurst to believe that one day America would "show itself equal to the whole of that commerce which now attracts the envy of the world." In fact, Bathurst had lived to see the portentous growth of America, and Burke concludes, he would be "fortunate indeed if he lives to see nothing that shall vary the prospect and cloud the setting of his day" (Virgil, *Fourth Ecologue*).

There is no mistaking the occular imagery here: the passage is replete with references to views, vision, foreseeing, seeing, scenes, gazing, and prospects. The aim is to portray the colonial problem in a particular fashion and to encourage a specific approach to its resolution. If the Ministry could see with Burke's eyes, it would discover the problem to be located not in America, but in English policy. Again, the insistent empiricism that marks so much of the speech here provides a standard for judgment. The perspective that Burke would have his audience assume apprehends the historical sweep of circumstance. Unlike North's "contracted" vision, Burke's can discern the true nature of America's past. Only this expansive vision could finally realize that "Whatever England has been growing into by a progressive increase of improvement, brought in by varieties of people, by a succession of civilizing conquests, and civilizing settlements in a series of seventeen hundred years, you shall see as much added to her by America in the course of a single life."

As if to focus the perspective he would induce, Burke insists upon unveiling the particular features and details of the colonial problem. Though perhaps taxing, the strategy is deliberate; Burke is relentless, because "generalities, which in all other cases are apt to heighten and raise the subject, have here a tendency to sink it. When we speak of commerce with out colonies, fiction lags behind truth, invention is unfruitful, and imagination cold and barren." By implication, Burke opponents, enamored as they are of "abstract ideas" and "general theories," are blind to the realities of the situation. The blindness prohibited the Ministry from seeing a fundamental shift in the nature of Anglo-American relations. Attention to actual circumstances would have allowed the Ministry to see what colonial wealth meant. Now, the commonplace image of parent-child relations reverses its own terms. Once descriptive of English primacy, the familial metaphor had, in the face of material conditions, yielded to a greater reality. "For some time past," Burke explains, "the old world has been fed from the new. The scarcity which you have felt would have been a desolating famine, if this child of your old age, with a true filial piety, with a Roman charity, had not put the full breast of its youthful exuberance to the mouth of its exhausted parent." In addition to its striking reversal of a complacent image, the passage is important for its appeal to the Cymon and Xanthippe legend. Like Cymon, England had become virtually dependent upon its own child and so can no longer act as it once did. This is a lesson generated from observation, not theory, and illustrated with recourse to an ancient legend. Once again Burke has reconstituted from the past a rationale for judgment and action in the present.

Fixed within this exemplary perspective, Burke is better able to understand the prospects before him. He can articulate in principle his objection to specific proposals. These proposals are met with a series of maxims, but maxims rooted in experience and not in "mere general theories." Properly grounded axioms are to be distinguished above all for their social utility; they are expedient precisely because they recognize the needs of the community and provide the principles of action necessary to meet them. Abstract theorizing, on the other hand, is marked by artifice and impracticality; it is overly rationalistic and hence cannot account for the variety of human experience and collective values. The effect of Burke's brief refutation is to trump North's self-avowed interest in the common good and to expose North's bill as faulty on both the level of principle and the level of expedience. Burke confesses that his opinion is "much more in favor of prudent management than of force,—considering force not as an odious, but a feeble, instrument for preserving a people so numerous, so active, so growing, so spirited as this."

A series of four objections make up Burke's challenge to North's bill. Though brief, each carries the weight of a principle achieved through experience. The use of force, which North's bill assumes, can only be temporary, for "a nation is not governed which perpetually is to be conquered." Force is also by nature uncertain, for "terror is not always the effect of force; and an armament is not always a victory." Again, force impairs the "object by your very endeavor to preserve it," and Burke says, "I do not choose wholly to break the American spirit; because it is that spirit which has made the country." Finally and summarily, Burke objects to its lack of precedent. The English experience in America has in fact been pacific: "Our ancient indulgence has been said to be pursued to a fault. It may be so; but we know, if feeling is evidence, that our fault was more tolerable than our attempt to mend it, and our sin far more salutary than our penitence." The objections are then enclosed with an appeal to principle, simultaneously buttressed by material evidence and expedience. The accumulated effect of these maxims adds weight to Burke's argument generally; but they also enhance our view of Burke's reflective judgment. The maxims by which North's policy is refuted come at the end of a long series of factual observations—they do not precede those observations. Burke's argument is thus more than stringently inductive, it negotiates a path between reductive theorizing and sheer facticity. The structure of the argument itself reveals Burke's domain of judgment between the general and the particular; and North's agenda, as a result, is more visibly impoverished for its failure to occupy similar ground. It is instructed by empty theory, is artificial, without precedent, ignorant of the past, and therefore cannot sustain its own claims to expediency. Burke's proposal, conversely, is revealed to be anchored in principle and experience and is therefore practical as well as virtuous. Burke's account of America's material wealth ends at the level of principle and so enacts the process and form of judgment he would have his audience assume. The factual and material basis of such judgment in turn provides a transition into Burke's second account, now describing the American character and its resistance to arbitrary rule. This second narrative is in fact more interpretive and less detailed than the former, but borrows from it the standards and posture of empirical judgment. Burke can thereby exploit the yield from his first narrative to illustrate the dominant, yet ineffable, feature of the Americans, their "fierce spirit of liberty." Here too the account reveals a kind of judging about judgment, a speech both referential and self-referential, which characterizes the oration as a whole. As such, the narration induces a historical perspective by showing the narrator to be infused with historical understanding. Burke so promises to "lay open" the causes of this American spirit and to reveal the appropriate response.

Chief among the reasons for this spirit is its genesis in the English past. But the past in this sense is not taken as a distant object; it is, rather, close by and inevitable. "Abstract liberty," Burke explains, "like other mere abstraction, is not to be found." Instead, "liberty inheres in some sensible object," and America, like England, locates its freedom in the issue of taxation." Like most such problems, the question of taxation is understandable only in terms of its historical placement and precedent and is resolvable only in those terms. In fact, Burke writes, "on this point of taxes the ablest pens and most eloquent tongues have been exercised, the greatest spirits have acted and suffered." Such experience, moreover, is made accessible and current by its presence in common law and lore. The right to grant monies—in effect to tax themselves—the colonists found sanctioned in the English Constitution and acknowledged in "ancient parchments." In addition to its genesis in the English past, as a result of it, the very right to self-taxation had developed into a principle of immediate relevance. In much the same way as Burke's account of American circumstances progressed from fact to principle, so this account propels the American question from its basis in past experience toward its resolution in principle. Even as Burke attacks the Ministry's appeal to abstractions and empty theories of right, he seeks to legitimize the colonial appeal to the principle of self-taxation. The Americans, Burke explains, understood as "a fundamental principle, that in all monarchies the people must in effect themselves, mediately or immediately, possess the power of granting their own money, or no shadow of liberty could exist." Unlike North's policy, this was a principle resulting from experience, not ancillary to it.

A similar movement characterizes Burke's portrait of religion in America. The American character had been shaped by Americans' flight from England; as a result their particular faith is the "dissidence of dissent and the Protestantism of the Protestant." The American education system, similarly, by nature resists ill-suited government; its emphasis upon legal training ought to be warning enough to the current ministry: "*Abeunt studia in mores.*" The Americans, as a necessary result, are well equipped to "augur misgovernment at a distance and snuff the approach of tyranny in every tainted breeze." Finally, the very physical character of Anglo-American relations thwarts arbitrary rule. The "disobedient spirit of the colonies," Burke explains, is due in part to the brute fact that they are separated from the mother country by an ocean. Simple as that fact is, it predicates an important principle of government: "In large bodies the circulation of power must be less vigorous at the extremities. Nature has said it." Thus the proximity of fact and principle, consonant with the relationship between past and present, issues an unmistakable directive. Failing to engage its policy with such standards, the Ministry invites disaster. The past, Burke concludes, will inevitably make itself felt; and the American spirit of liberty "has grown with the growth of the people in your colonies, and increased with the increase of their wealth: a spirit that unhappily meeting with an exercise of power in England, which, however lawful, is not reconciled to any idea of liberty, much less with theirs, has kindled this flame that is ready to consume us."

Argument

Thus forewarned, the audience is now in a position, if not to accept, at least to envision a new course of action. The ensuing forty-seven paragraphs detail Burke's alternative; but more than a series of policy suggestions, this is a lesson in judgment. Burke has earlier exposed, and will again, the impotence of theory to accommodate material problems. Here he demonstrates the utility of historical understanding and, as he does so, reveals the proper grounds for action and judgment. As the paragraphs unfold, we see the past and its constraints laying a foundation for Burke, directing his perspective as he would have it shape ours. It is a pragmatic view, tending toward the general and didactic. This section of the speech summarizes and enacts the principles previously introduced. As Burke in turn establishes the conditions of judgment, surveys possible courses of action, and finally arrives at his proposition, we witness again discourse about judgment that is itself exemplary.

As with all successful arguments from exclusion, Burke's concludes with a sense of inevitability. His position assumes the strength of logical necessity. But in addition to this somewhat transparent achievement, Burke's argument has advanced with a subtle but irresistible progress. The speech has thus far ascribed to experience and past fact a compelling, immediate force. Now, coupling historical to logical necessity, Burke aligns rational and moral imperatives in the service of his argument.

Careful to make clear what his proposal is not, Burke introduces the bill with a now familiar insistence upon its practical appeal. As he begins, one fact is clear: the source of America's complaint is its exclusion from British standards of liberty; that complaint, in turn, stems from the issue of taxation. The sheer reality of this fact sets in relief North's abstraction into theory a concrete problem. Indeed, the fashionable tendency to locate the issue in questions of right is just such an abstraction. It therefore fails to meet the problem on its own terms and has rendered Anglo-American relations unnaturally complex. Burke promises to take the opposite course, and while admitting that "gentlemen of profound learning are fond of displaying" their concern for the question of right, he observes the baneful effects. Like Milton's vision of hell (*Paradise Lost*, 592–94), Burke finds such idle speculation to be "the great Serbonian bog / Betwixt Damiata and Mount Cassius old / Where whole armies have sunk."

In refusing to entertain the question of right, however, Burke does not so much ignore the problem as render it irrelevant. Over against this abstract—and therefore inappropriate—consideration, Burke's approach is unabashedly "narrow, confined, and wholly limited to the policy of the question." This insistence upon the practical ends of any given question allows Burke to engage the problem morally but not abstractly, concretely but not pedantically. Burke can now claim without inconsistency that it "is not what a lawyer tells me I may do, but what humanity, reason, and justice tell me I ought to do." Here the appeal to circumstances and principled response conflates motives to honor and expedience, fusing particular facts within a general perspective. Although brief, this passage is propaedeutic to the remainder of the speech; and by establishing this calculus as the basis of judgment, Burke provides a standard by which to judge not only his resolutions but those of his opponents. Unlike the North administration, Burke concludes, "I am not determining a point of law, I am restoring tranquility; and the general character and situation of a people must determine what sort of government is fitted for them. That point nothing else can or ought to determine."

Burke proposes first to "admit the people of our colonies into an interest in the constitution." The record of North's administration, and indeed all ministries since Rockingham's, had made clear the folly of excluding colonists from English privileges. As Burke reviews that record, he again exposes North's administration not only as governing with impunity, but as failing even to meet its avowed ends. The policy of the current Ministry was neither honorable nor expedient, "no more than suspicions, conjectures, deviations, formed in defiance of fact and experience." In lines that recall the *ingratio*, Burke contrasts his own perspective to that of North and thereby signals the progress of the speech thus far. Burke claims to have assumed that "frame of mind which was the most natural and the most reasonable" and to have sought a "total renunciation of every speculation of my own." He had thereby come to realize that the only possible solution was to allow the colonists into the ancient constitution—into the English past. As Burke concludes the paragraph, he at once summarizes the tenets of his speech and prepares for their demonstration. This section again, like all preceding divisions, eventuates in principles that unify the speech even as it shifts direction and function. Its concluding lines are familiar enough, and they again show Burke to be acting "with a profound reverence for the wisdom of our ancestors, who have left us the inheritance of so happy a constitution and so flourishing an empire, and, what is a thousand times more valuable, the treasury of the maxims and principles which formed the one and obtained the other."

Resolutions

We are not surprised, therefore, when Burke announces his resolutions by first explaining how he arrived at them. It is this process of discovery and insight that Burke would have others follow and that functions synecdochically as a standard of Whig political judgment.

At this moment of crisis, Burke does not seek answers in the fanciful and speculative texts of Plato, More, or Harrington. His plan, far from utopian, is "before me; it is at my feet,—And the rude swain / Treads daily on it with his clouted shoon" (Milton, *Comus*, 634–35). Like most of his allusions, this Miltonic image serves to imbed Burke's argument historically and to convey a sense of homely, sublunar wisdom. In fact Burke is willing to go no further in search of theoretical justification than "the ancient constitutional policy of this kingdom." Burke's argument mimes the character of the Constitution insofar as both are constrained by the historical development of principle. As to his resolutions generally, there can be no mistaking their source and legitimacy: "return to that mode," Burke advises, "which a uniform experience has marked out to you as best, and in which you walked with security, advantage and honor, until the year 1763."

Taken together, Burke's six primary resolutions are meant to grant colonists the right to self-taxation and to expose the poverty of North's program. But each resolution is so composed as to repeat under different guises the same rationale for action and adjudication. Each specific claim is anchored in historical fact, and together "these solid truths compose six fundamental propositions." As such, they are objective and compelling. "The propositions," Burke says, "are all mere matters of fact; and if they are such facts as draw irresistible conclusions even in the stating, this is the power of truth, and not any management of mine." Each resolution thereby assumes the moral and logical necessity of historical truth. Burke proposes first only that the colonists have not in the past had access to representation. This, Burke claims, "is a plain matter of fact, necessary to be laid down, and . . . it is laid down in the language of the constitution." The second resolution appeals to a similar facticity: the colonists have been unjustly taxed, thereby grieved, and ultimately incited to resistance. This conclusion, of course, is less certifiable in factual terms, but the historical appeal upon which it is based by now lends it credence. Burke meets the problems of the past with constitutional measures generated from the past. Thus Burke exercises the historical force of the Constitution, conceived as "the genuine produce of the ancient, rustic, manly, homebred sense of this country,—I dare not rub off a particle of the venerable rust that rather adorns and preserves, than destroys, the metal." By participating in the construction of the past, Burke's resolutions evoke its authority and so claim an independent moral status. "Determining to fix articles of peace," Burke concludes, "I was resolved not to be wise beyond what was written." This, he says, "if it be not ingenious, I am sure is safe." Resolutions three and four—

that no adequate system of representation has yet been devised for the colonies, and that the colonists themselves possess the means for such representation—Burke likewise asserts as facts. So too is the fifth a "resolution of fact" meant to point out the precedent for colonial grants in lieu of external taxation. The final resolution becomes an inevitable result of the preceding "facts." Burke asks his audience to recognize that in the past—before the ascendency of North—grants from the colonies were beneficial to both America and England. "The conclusion," Burke insists, "is irresistible." Thus assent to historical fact becomes a basis for action and justification of Whig policy.

Burke's transition into the corollary resolutions repeats the controlling movement of the speech, now familiar as a progression from fact to principle to fact. Here again Burke exercises his irresistible conclusion to direct the terms of the following arguments. "The question now," Burke says, "on all the accumulated matter, is,—whether you will choose to abide by a profitable experience, or a mischievous theory; whether you choose to build on imagination or fact; whether you prefer enjoyment of hope; satisfaction in your subjects or discontent?" These corollary resolutions call for repeal of George III's various and recent coercive bills in order to restore the tranquility Burke remembers in the days of Rockingham power. As with the primary resolutions, Burke appeals to historical sanction, principles that owe their authority not to abstract ideas of right but to their proven utility. "Man acts from adequate motives relative to his interest," Burke concludes, "and not on metaphysical speculation. Aristotle, the great master of reasoning tells us, and with great weight and propriety, to be wary against this species of delusive geometrical accuracy in moral arguments, as the most fallacious of all sophistry." This demand for English rights at the expense of English peace was precisely the problem with North's policy. The Rockingham Whigs, conversely, had employed a different, more effective calculus. During their ministries "everything was sweetly and harmoniously disposed," and Burke can only lament that the empire was then "more united than it is now, or than it is likely to be by the present methods."

Refutation

The speech shifts now into a refutative phase, but the attack is only an extension of the principles generated thus far. Burke's refutation of North's plan is clustered around four points: First, the plan is a "thing new, unheard of, support by no experience, justified by no analogy, without example of our ancestors or root in the constitution"; second, the plan encourages court influence, and therefore imperils the constitution itself; third, the plan cannot possibly achieve its avowed ends; and finally, the plan can only magnify logistical difficulties and so create greater discord. Given the nature of North's plan, Burke asks his audience to behold the differences. As he contrasts the two plans, we are provided a virtual summary of Burke's argument, employed to vanquish North's bill and vindicate Rockingham policy. The contrast, moreover, articulates a rationale for action in which Burke shapes ministerial policy into an immanent and insidious force, tolerated at the cost of imperial disaster. Burke's proposal is "plain and simple; the other full of perplexed and intricate mazes. This is mild, that harsh; this is found by experience effectual for its purposes; the other is a new project. This is universal,—the other calculated for certain colonies only; this is immediate in its conciliatory operation; the other is remote, contingent, full of hazard. Mine is what becomes the dignity of a ruling people— gratuitous, unconditional, and not held out as a matter of bargain and sale. I have done my duty in proposing it to you."

Because the tone of the final sentence differs so markedly from its preceding lines, it is worth considering in greater detail. The sentence comes at the end of a series of antithetical constructions and lends closure to the argument. But the sentiment is more important for its moral implications: in declaring his obligations satisfied, Burke shifts attention from the issues specifically toward his character generally. In doing so, he established the terms of his conclusion. Burke now exercises fully the principles he has so far invoked and demonstrated, creating a vision of political order along notably Rockinghamite lines. Apologizing for the length of the speech, Burke nevertheless insists that "this is the misfortune of those to whose influence nothing will be conceded, and who must win every inch of their ground by argument." Here a thinly disguised attack on privilege and court influence tells us more than what the passage may suggest ostensibly. It is, of course, consistent with Burke's long-standing suspicion of the "King's friends." But the lines also indicate something of the Rockingham Whigs and indeed of Burke himself. Long divested of its ties to the court, the party had been forced upon its own resources since the ascension of George III. Burke's party, when it had failed, did so through a failure to act decisively. As its representative, Burke has undertaken through his speech to correct his party's malaise, to give it voice and direction, and ultimately to vindicate its principles. What Burke says of himself, therefore, may be understood as a reflection upon the Rockingham legacy. "I have this comfort," Burke concludes, "that in every stage of the American affairs I have steadily opposed the measures that have produced the confusion, and may bring on the destruction, of this empire. I now go so far as to risk a proposal of my own. If I cannot give peace to my country, I give it to my conscience."

Peroration

The conclusion of Burke's speech, we now understand, is to be more than a summary of its parts. It is a consummation of its action into principle. Arguments have been interwoven with appeals to both honor and expedience, themselves now indistinguishable. This conflation has been achieved through a long series of structural permutations, wherein facts blur into truths, and circumstances into maxims. Once established, the principles direct our apprehension of history. In this fashion Burke exploits the evidentiary force of material circumstances and the moral force of historically ground truths to create a prospect of compelling rhetorical force. "As long as you have the wisdom to keep the sovereign authority of this country as the sanctuary of liberty, the sacred principle consecrated to our common faith, wherever the chosen race and sons of England worship freedom, they will turn their faces toward you." Burke thus vanquishes North's program, placing in its stead a plan principled but not impractical, expedient but not unjust. He has demonstrated exemplary judgment, creating a perspective capable of taking in historical truth as well as current expedients. It is within this perspective that Burke commands his advisory appeal. The speech has been a lesson in reading history, and if it is a decidedly Rockingham history, nevertheless it articulates its ideals at a moment of crisis. Burke's history, like the form and character of his oration, is a composite of carefully designed images, allusions, and progressions. As such it may well be nostalgic, but it is nevertheless available for those who would learn and act upon its truths. Burke's history is an appealing one, peopled by the likes of Horace, Milton, Aristotle, Ovid, and Virgil. From such luminaries Burke sought to enlighten a people seemingly blind to their own past. The rhetorical accomplishment of Burke's speech is its identification of history with Whig history and the lessons of the past with the advisory function of his argument. Most important, perhaps, Burke understood that to represent history was not enough—that to make history present one had in effect to be history. The *Speech on Conciliation* is ultimately an act of exemplary understanding, a process in which venerable truths are situated within immediate political contexts. There will be those who, like the current Ministry, neglect the truths of history. But "to men truly initiated and rightly taught, these ruling and master principles, which in the opinion of such men as I have mentioned have no substantial existence, are in truth everything and all in all."

The movement of Burke's oration has been conducted along several levels of progression. Clearly the ostensible form of the speech is indebted to classical models; the speech may be seen as an example of conventional form in the service of an argument from history. At this level the speech suggests a rational consistency and structure in keeping with Burke's purposes. The meaning of the oration cannot be fully apprehended, however, unless we attend to its more subtle progression through temporal and conceptual phases. Here Burke charts a movement from past to present to future as a means of grounding principles of judgment in human experience. These temporal phases thus embody conditions of past fact, the axiomatic basis of political decision, and a rationale for deliberative action. So ordered, Burke's oration offers to both immediate and historical audiences a standard for rhetorical judgment.

The *Speech on Conciliation*, finally, may be seen as a practical extension of the principles Burke would celebrate. Certainly the speech is notable for its wealth of imagery and aesthetic appeal. It is more significant that its meaning is constituted as a form of discursive action and requires, for its completion, the exercise of rhetorical judgment. Burke's audience, however expansive and however distant, is nevertheless obligated to understand the oration in its capacity as an audience, to apprehend its meaning according to the standards of human community and practical reason. As an exemplary exercise in rhetorical judgment, Burke's oration is able to reconfigure human experience free from the constraints of the moment and the burdens of speculative principle. From the perspective it induces, we are thus led to see in the *Speech on Conciliation* an example of what it means to deliberate wisely.

4

Speech to the Electors of Bristol
The Space of Rhetorical Virtue

Burke's 1775 performance put on display standards of reason he thought appropriate to the exercise of political virtue. As might be expected, however, the speaker found himself confronted in the years ahead with alternative conceptions of just what qualified as virtuous action. His own exercise of political judgment was repeatedly called into question, and as his career developed, Burke became something of a specialist in the ancient rhetorical arts of self-defense. But whatever pain such challenges brought to Burke, they obliged him to articulate time and again principles which he believed to be basic to the proper conduct of politics. We are fortunate, therefore, in having access to a discourse constantly under strain, an advocate ceaselessly promoting and attempting to act upon standards of virtue as he understood them.

Burke's *Speech to the Electors of Bristol*[1] represents a high point—if not for the fortunes of the speaker, then for those who would trace the career of virtue as a political and rhetorical construction. The Bristol address gives pointed expression to problems only hinted at in the *Speech on Conciliation* and elaborates upon issues not heretofore fully developed. In particular, the Bristol address focuses upon the space of virtue, that political and psychological realm where actors are free to exercise rhetorical judgment—even as they accept the possibility of their own removal. Here Burke gave rhetorical force to a conception of virtue rooted in civic vision, a capacity on the part of speaker and community alike to see beyond the sweep of immediate events and toward the greater good.[2]

In the autumn of 1780, Burke confided to the Duke of Portland that he hoped never to "reject the principles of general public prudence." What precisely Burke meant by such principles he does not here say. He is, however, eager to declare what they do not entail. "But as to leaving to the crowd," Burke continues, "to choose for me, what principles I ought to hold, or what course I ought to pursue for their benefit—I had much rather innocently and obscurely, mix with them . . . than to betray them by learning lessons from them. They are naturally proud, tyrannical, and ignorant; bad scholars and worse masters."[3] These are not, by our reckoning, the sentiments of enlightened leadership; they are in fact familiar as objects of assault on Burke's conservatism. While I have no particular interest in either defending or promoting Burke's conservatism—the term seems hopelessly anachronistic in any case—we cannot simply ignore this apparent disdain for "the crowd." The question of Burke's commitment to public politics is a real one—certainly more real than whether or not he represents the founding of modern conservatism. Fortunately, we have in Burke's *Speech to the Electors of Bristol* (1780) an oration rich enough to yield some answers and complex enough to discourage its reduction to ideological fodder.

Delivered before his supporters in Bristol's Guildhall, the *Speech to the Electors of Bristol* stands as one of Burke's earliest and most fully developed accounts of his political principles. As a campaign address, it is perhaps challenged in the English language only by Lincoln's for scope of allusion and depth of insight. But as a campaign address, it invited, as might be expected, both applause and condemnation. In its review of the published version, the *Monthly Review* noted that Burke "gives so clear, so manly, so convincing a defense of his principles and proceedings, as cannot, in our opinion, fail of extorting the warmest applause from every generous, candid, liberal mind."[4] Others were less impressed by Burke's lofty pronouncements in place of political action and found him "steadily pursuing that pernicious maxim, of not obeying the voice of his constituents." Burke himself was content to note only that the speech "was well received, and made a marked impression—they [his managers] found a turn in the minds of even the lowest of the populace." In fact the Bristol address is much more suggestive than any of these accounts; it provides us an extraordinary opportunity to see Burke formulating and promoting a set of principles meaningful only within the terms of the speech act itself. This meaning is achieved as it negotiates a series of conceptual tensions or conventional disjuncts: text and context, particular and general, expedience and principle. Fully realized, the Bristol address dramatically enacts its own claims to represent a discourse of virtue. Because this process requires that

Burke respond to and reshape specific historical circumstances, to them we now turn.

The 1770s were years of relative success for Burke. In opposition for the entire decade, he nevertheless thrived in a volatile climate of ministerial change, imperial frictions, party contest, and parliamentary dispute. When in late 1774 he could no longer be supported in his Wendover seat, Burke was obliged to seek election elsewhere. A seat had been arranged for him in Malton, to which he was initially committed. At the last moment, however, Burke was informed that, through a variety of circumstances, Bristol could be had. Burke could not refuse. Bristol was England's second city, an important mercantile and shipping center, and a regional center of political power. Literally dashing off to the port city, Burke arrived after the poll had been opened. Along with fellow Whig Henry Cruger, he emerged a winner, but already portents of struggle were becoming evident. Burke refused to indulge his electors with a victory parade, and he made no effort to accommodate Cruger, whom he disdained as a lazy and incompetent opportunist. More significant in the long run, Burke made it clear in his speech of thanks that he was laboring under no mandate. On 3 November Burke explained his position. A representative must be sensible to the needs of his constituents: "but his unbiased opinion, his mature judgment, his enlightened conscience, he ought not to sacrifice to you, to any man, or to any set of men living." Burke continued unabashed, "Your representative owes you, not his industry only, but his judgment; and he betrays, instead of serving you, if he sacrifices it to your opinion."

This was neither the first nor last time Burke was to make explicit such views. His *Letter to the Sheriffs of Bristol* (1777) may be read as an extended justification for acting on precisely the assumptions stated above.[5] From the beginning of the decade to the end of his life, from *Discontents* to *Letters on a Regicide Peace,* Burke's discourse was tirelessly apologiac. His sometimes shrill and anguished, sometimes brilliant attempts to acquit himself before history represent some of the most sophisticated examples of apologia in the language. Even as we note the increasing sophistication of this discourse, however, we must appreciate the very real and practical issues to which it gives expression. The *Speech to the Electors of Bristol* in 1780 is theoretically of interest, not because it transcends the particular, but because it so integrates immediate concerns as to give new meaning to general principles. The most significant of these theoretical statements regards the space of virtue; Burke is here concerned to establish the grounds of proper judgment. He finds it in a deliberative realm between the press of popular sentiment—which is volatile, shifting, and immediate—and the cold abstractions of reason—which are aloof, unsituated, and irrelevant to the demands of public life. What this space looks like and what it requires in the way of civic responsibility are questions that can be answered only as we attend to the speech closely and with patience.[6]

All told, Burke visited Bristol exactly twice in the six years following his election. Even by the relatively casual standards of eighteenth-century politics, that record seemed to many rather under the mark. This is not to say that Burke was unaware of or uninterested in his constituency; as he explained it, he was so busy in attending to their needs that he had neither time nor will to visit them regularly. However plausible, this kind of argument has its limits, and the people of Bristol seemed to require more attention than Burke was willing to grant. It is not enough, however, to explain Burke's predicament on this basis alone. More fundamental and more damning evidence against Burke's tenure as their representative could be readily marshaled.

To begin with, Burke's sympathy for American interests had seemed excessive, especially as those interests impinged on Bristol's commercial prospects. To many, Burke was guilty of misplacing his patriotic zeal; did not Bristol's trade concerns trump colonial declarations of right? Burke had gone over much of this ground three years earlier in the *Letter to the Sheriffs of Bristol*, but recent shifts in the fortunes of the British army, and a turn of events in Bristol's own commercial life, required that Burke account again for his pro-American activities. The Bristol address makes clear that this was no easy task, in part because Bristol had been so immediately affected by colonial embargoes and in part because its famous representative had not bothered to visit the city since 1776.

On a related issue Burke was equally vulnerable. Trade restrictions on Irish goods had long worked to the decided advantage of Bristol merchants. While hardly revolutionary, the changes brought about in the late years of the decade relieved some of the burdens on Irish manufactures. The process by which these changes were brought was complex and politically sensitive. A number of issues combined to provide a compelling rationale for easing restrictions: the threat of Irish revolt, the fears that Irish problems might play into the hands of American and French designs, and the genuine concern for imperial justice on the part of the Ministry. Needless to say, Bristol merchants felt slighted and detected in Burke's support for Irish relief additional evidence of misplaced sympathies and twisted priorities.

Adding fuel to the merchants' complaint was Burke's support for a debtor's relief bill recently presented by Lord Beauchamp. In a city of merchants, credit concerns were naturally crucial, and they saw in Beauchamp's bill a direct threat to the economic interests of the community. The bill sought to repeal exceedingly harsh punishments for default—including life imprisonment—and to rewrite inequitable procedures of trial. Burke was, moreover, accused of treating Bristol's petition against the bill with contempt in the House of Commons. Burke had indeed supported the bill and, while recognizing its faults, was wholly in sympathy with its aims. The bill, in any case, failed to pass, but Burke's management of Bristol's interests was still very much on the minds of the Bristol citizenry.

Of all the charges advanced against Burke, the fourth and final was most pressing. Burke had, it was charged, proved much too conciliatory to recent Catholic relief measures. In May 1778, George Savile's Catholic Relief Act repealed a few of the more notorious laws in the generally notorious Irish Penal Code. In particular, Saville's act removed statutes from 1699 prohibiting Catholic ownership of property and restriction against Catholic education. In addition to antagonizing general anti-Catholic sentiment, Burke's support for the measure, and indeed his long-standing efforts on behalf of religious tolerance, invited attacks from Bristol's Dissenting population.

Putting an edge on all of this were the anti-Catholic disturbances of June 1780. On 29 May George Gordon announced to assembled members of the Protestant Association "That the whole body of the Protestant Association do attend in Saint George's fields, on Friday the next, at ten o'clock in the morning," and from there march "to the House of Commons for the delivery of the Protestant petition."[7] The march precipitated one of the most explosive and bloody instances of domestic unrest of the century. When it was finally over, hundreds lay dead and total casualties amounted to well over four hundred. Houses were sacked and burned, Newgate Prison was seized and opened, distilleries drained. Burke's home was threatened and put under guard; others associated with the relief measures suffered directly from the pillage. On Friday, 2 June, Parliament itself was briefly besieged by "several thousand" angry followers of Gordon. Something of Burke's immediate response can be indicated from the report of the *General Evening Post*. Burke, the newspaper noted on 6 June, "felt so much for the debased dignity of Parliament at that moment, that he lost all temper, and bitterly lamented the fate of such times, when those who pretended to be the advocates of freedom, were establishing the most wretched slavery—a bludgeoned mob and an armed soldiery!"[8]

Against this backdrop of war, commercial strain, and sectarian violence, Burke's Bristol address stands in dramatic contrast. Its steady course of reason, its way of highlighting its own control over ideas and images, its very prudence, and its tone and texture give to the oration an exemplary force that serves as a symbolic corrective to the disorder and fanaticism that in part constitute its subject matter.

Burke's Bristol address thus comes at a poignant moment, a turning point in his career located amid crises of state. It comes, moreover, just as British politics wavers between the reform pressure of the bourgeoisie and the traditional prerogatives of the aristocracy. Nowhere is this tension more palpable than in the argument about the role of the representative. At least since the Wilkes controversy of 1769, the idea that a representative might rightfully exercise his judgment independent of the expressed wishes of the community had become a matter of heated controversy. The representative, many argued, ought to receive and act upon the instructions of his constituency; to do otherwise was to abrogate a basic political trust.

Burke faced a challenge as an individual, as a representative for Bristol, and as a symbol, an image of an established but increasingly unpopular paradigm of legislative judgment. Even the most cursory reading of the address indicates that Burke grapples with both problems. On its surface, the Bristol address clearly partitions itself into five sections, each treating an ostensibly different theme. The brief introduction expressly addresses the main principle, as the orator explains the benefits of independent judgment in politics. The next four sections, following in the sequence of a well-ordered brief, respond to the specific charges—that Burke had neglected his constituents, had acted against their interests in the matter of Irish trade policy, had ignored their clearly voiced sentiment in supporting Beauchamp's bill to reform penalties against debtors, and had offended public opinion in supporting Saville's measures for relief of Roman Catholics.

Under more careful scrutiny, however, the local movement among discrete arguments gives way to a different and more general pattern of development. The four sections constituting the body of the speech appear less as self-contained arguments than as narratives that repeatedly instantiate principles announced in the introduction. These four "stories" provide a series of disclosures, each meant to vindicate Burke's principles by revealing their successful operation in action, each meant to illuminate Burke's actions by reference to a single set of principles incarnated in different circumstances. Taken separately, the narratives unfold along conventional lines, framing situations and events within historical boundaries. Taken together, they move in a slow, inexorable circle, as they loop back to their genesis in principle and thereby clarify moments of exemplary judgment. The movement of the text is accordingly complex, its course determined by the braided threads of principle and action, by the interlocking structures of political time and space.

Analysis of the Speech

Burke's introductory remarks quickly and efficiently establish the parameters of the situation. Faced with the demands of the election and uncertain of its outcome, Burke is politician enough to realize he must reclaim popular support. He desires, therefore, to "take the authentic sense of my friends upon a business of so much delicacy." In fact, public opinion will determine whether Burke continues the canvass at all; he will, at all events, respect the wishes of the electorate. This nod toward his audience, however, is immediately succeeded by a resolute claim to retain autonomy in judging deliberative issues. Even as Burke identifies his relationship to the city as that of "an honest servant in the equity of a candid and discerning master," he insists that his role is not one of obsequious dependence. As a representative called to account for his actions, he disdains the opportunity for apology or excuse and moves instead into the objective light of public space, a realm where all can judge for themselves what character discloses. This strategic move has its personal dimension; Burke was not by temperament inclined toward the hurly-burly of campaign politics. Earlier, he had explained to Portland that "oldish men are not more fit to court the people than the Ladies—nor is it very becoming—Turpe senex Miles, turpe senilis Amor." Such private predilections need not qualify the public point, however. Burke is adamant in either case to set the terms of his own account, and from the outset he refuses to explain away his behavior. "I have lived too long to be served by apologies," he says, "or to stand in need of them. The part I have acted has been in open day; and to hold out to a conduct which stands in that clear and steady light for all its good and all its evil, to hold out to that conduct the paltry winking tapers of excuses—I will never do it." We note, even at this early moment in the address, a pattern of images that facilitate the argument; actions are explicable as they are public and must be evaluated in the light of public reason. Others, he declares, "may obscure it with their smoke, but they never can illumine sunshine by such flame as theirs." This light-dark imagery continues to assist the speaker's account of himself throughout the oration. More than a conventional set of metaphoric clusters, they shape and give expression to the values Burke would have his audience assume.

Burke's opening lines, moreover, set into play conceptual tensions that define political judgment. Prompted by circumstances to solicit popular support, the representative appeals to a principle of autonomy by nature resistant to such endorsement. This recourse to principle in the face of political flux characterizes the opening stage of the text's development. The tone here is dignified and distant, and if Burke acknowledges the interests of his constituents, he just as strongly insists upon the limits of their claim. Amid the push of events and the pull of strident opinions, an unchecked desire to satisfy popular appetites reveals weakness, not strength of character. The representative, rather, must "look to the nature of things" and not to the "humors of men." Only then is he in a position to act in accord with the natural rhythms of time, liberated from the short-lived demands of popular whim. Indeed, Burke stresses, the "very attempt towards pleasing everybody discovers a temper always flashy, and often false and insincere. Therefore, as I have proceeded straight onward in my conduct, so I will proceed in my account of those parts of it which have been most excepted to." This stance, in turn, requires stability of character and conduct, and as Burke has acted, so shall he account for his actions.

As he prepares to undertake this disclosure, Burke effects an important redefinition of the role of public judgment: denied the right to restrain the autonomy of the representative directly, his audience assumes the role of spectators; they are to render a judgment only at the end of the performance. Whereas in *Discontents* Burke was concerned to establish a collaborative relationship with his audience, here he works to situate it within a different interpretive frame. In both cases Burke's rhetoric creates for the speaker an exemplary role; here that role is more explicitly self-regarding. "Applaud us when we run," Burke directs his hearers, "console us when we fall, cheer us when we recover; but let us pass on,—for God's sake let us pass on." Understanding this relation to the representative, the electors—like their representatives—judge from a distance, "like sound judges, and not like cavilling pettifoggers and quibling pleaders, prying into flaws and hunting for exceptions. Look, gentlemen to the whole tenor of your member's conduct."

In much the same sense, Burke argues that the preservation of the public space itself requires a perspective located at a proper degree of distance. It too is sensitive to the pressure of heteronomous opinion and threatens to collapse when popular demands overwhelm its borders. An arena of free action, this space is needed for the work of the representative; and those who most value this work "will not bear to have it soiled and impaired by those for whose sake they make a thousand sacrifices to preserve it immutable and whole." If the popular will intrudes too far into this space, if the representative becomes servile, then the space must contract, and the best men either will leave the public stage or seek refuge with the court. Again, Burke asks his audience to judge as he would judge and to maintain the necessary distance between the representative and the represented. "If we do not permit our members," he concludes, "to act upon a very enlarged view of things, we shall at length infallibly degrade our national representation into a confused and scuffling bustle of local agency. When the popular member is narrowed in his ideas and rendered timid in his proceedings, the service of the crown will be the sole nursery of statesmen." The first section of the speech thus ends where it started, anchored in principle to the autonomy of political judgment. And the multifaceted symmetry of the argument calls upon the auditors to adopt and act on the principle in question. In shifting their perspective from a restrictive view of heteronomous interest to an enlarged conception of political time and space, Burke sets up the possibility of his own vindication. Yet, since he asks the audience to act in emulation of his own judgment, he must disclose not only the principles that regulate his character, but his character as manifested in action.

The direction of the text shifts at this point. Burke now engages the specific charges outstanding against him, framing his response within a series of four narratives. The first of these concerns the most personal charge—that he neglected his Bristol constituents. Although brief, this section incorporates the spatial and temporal themes common to all the narratives.

Narrative 1: The Geography of Virtue

In a choice bit of understatement, Burke allows that "there is a decorum and propriety in a member of Parliament's paying a respectful court to his constituents." If he did not pay court often enough, however, it was not through lack of goodwill. Indeed, it was by virtue of the distance between Bristol and Westminster that Burke could attend to more important matters. Unlike his opponents, whose business seemed limited to shaking hands and making promises, Burke had exploited his opportunities in Parliament to advance the real interests of his constituents. "I canvassed you through your affairs," he explains, "not through your persons."

Apologia is as often as not an art of inversion, where issues of accusation are redirected into points of merit. Burke proves himself adept. The space between the representative and the represented is not, he explains, to be lamented, but to be protected against the seductions of the crowd and the pressures of campaign politics. Within this space, Burke's character is revealed in its fullness; though retaining the right to autonomous judgment, he remains alert to the legitimate interests of his constituents. "I was not only your representative as a body, I was the agent, the solicitor of individuals; I ran about wherever your affairs could call me; and in acting for you, I often appeared as a ship-broker than as a member of Parliament. There was nothing too laborious or too low for me to undertake."

Spatial distance, then, allows the representative freedom to use his time in the conduct of substantive business. More important, such distance opens a perspective on time necessary to the proper understanding of political realities. Burke admits that in fact he could have visited Bristol more often but chose not to do so. When the city was infused with the contagion of war against the colonies, and "all mounds and banks of our constancy were borne down at once, and the frenzy of the American war broke upon us like a deluge" Burke absented himself from Bristol. Why? From his more distant and more steady vantage, Burke could accurately gauge the situation; uncontaminated by this local frenzy, he understood the international repercussions of the war and found in every victory another goad to folly. Conversely, when his predictions proved correct and the war turned against England, Burke again chose to stay away, fearing to insult by his presence. "In this temper of yours and of my mind," he recalls, "I should sooner have fled to the extremities of the earth than have shown myself here." Yet, if his absence sometimes appeared indecorous, it proved exemplary in the end. Time has vindicated the representative's distance from the local and immediate, for it "at length has made us all of one opinion, and we have all opened our eyes on the true nature of the American war,—to the true nature of all its successes and all its failures." Viewed from the perspective of time present, the events of the past themselves, not apologies and excuses, justify Burke's stance. And as the audience participates in this narrative, it comes to share in its lesson—judgment must remain fixed in the nature of things: "This [is] a true, unvarnished, undisguised state of the affair. You will judge of it."

Narrative 2: Constancy as Virtue

The second narrative elaborates the lessons of the first. Burke's role in the Irish Trade Acts had seemed to many unduly sympathetic to the Irish, this at a time when Bristol's livelihood depended on its commercial relations. Burke, of course, was especially vulnerable on this matter; as a native of Ireland he inevitably risked offending the special interests of his adopted city. Nevertheless, Burke had sought to fix Anglo-Irish trade policy in a period of considerable unrest. The American war had opened up new markets and had forced a realignment of commercial relations. Confronted by a series of rapidly changing circumstances, Parliament wavered. Unable to chart a consistent or stable policy, it reacted blindly to each point of pressure. In prose that mimics the state of its subject, Burke recalled how Parliament was "frightened into a limited concession by the menaces of Ireland, frightened out of it by the menaces of England, was now frightened back again, and made a universal surrender of all that had been thought the peculiar, reserved, uncommunicable right of England." In the end came disaster: "A sudden light broke in upon us. It broke in, not through well-contrived and well-disposed windows, but through flaws and breaches—through the yawning chasms of our ruin. We were taught wisdom by humiliation." The power of the metaphor at the end of this passage contrasts significantly with the rapidly shifting syntax of its beginning. The style incorporates the point: the passage of time illuminates with unmistakable clarity the folly of mere temporizing.

Burke understood this principle before the event, and so he had stood firm amid the tumult. Not coincidentally, he remained distant from Bristol. Forgoing the "little, silly, canvass prattle of obeying instructions, and having no opinion but yours," Burke commanded a perspective denied to those sealed within the pressures of the moment. His distance offered a perspective for judgment that opened access to a higher order of reason. This enlarged view found warrant for action in "the instruction of truth and nature," and it secured its ends not by seducing public opinion, but by looking forward to the greater interests of the community. As Burke employed this enlarged view in the Irish Trade Acts debate, he once again provided an exemplar of sound political judgment. He thus drives home the point through a striking thematic and metaphoric summary: "A representative worthy of you ought to be a person of stability. I am to look, indeed, to your opinions,—but to such opinions as you and I must have five years hence. I was not to look to the flash of the day. I knew that you chose me, in my place, along with others, to be a pillar of the state, and not a weathercock on top of the edifice, exalted for my levity and versatility, and of no use but to indicate the shiftings of every fashionable gale."

Narrative 3: Virtue and Magnanimity

The third charge against Burke concerns Lord Beauchamp's bill, a measure designed to reduce the severity of penalties against debtors. As if to underscore the dangers of public seduction, this narrative reveals Burke to have acted in compliance with the short-sighted interests of the Bristol community. The city naturally had a stake in the strength of credit laws. It feared that Beauchamp's bill threatened the delicate balance between credit and capital and so presented to Burke a petition announcing its opposition. A rumor of sorts, we recall, suggested that Burke handled the petition with contempt. Not so, declared Burke. In fact, he had delivered the petition, "though it militated with my oldest and my most recent public opinions," with a "strong and more than usual recommendation to the consideration of the House, on account of the character and consequence of those who signed it." Ironically, then, Burke was chastised for something he had not done, and far from ignoring the wishes of his constituents, he had complied against his better judgment.

In the end, Burke could only regret he had not left himself open to criticism on the lesser matter. He had allowed sheer consensus to intrude on the integrity of this judgment, and for this he vowed compensation: "I owe what, if ever it be in my power, I shall most certainly pay,—ample atonement and usurious amends to liberty and humanity for my unhappy lapse."

Burke's failure to act on an enlarged view of the matter before him constituted a genuine failure of the public trust. Viewed dispassionately, Burke explained, the bill was just, designed only to remedy "a gross and cruel fault in our laws." And the very injustice of existing laws perpetuated foolish and inexpedient policies. Most notable among these were "acts of grace," whereby imprisoned debtors were released periodically solely because of overcrowding. The laws thus made a mockery of themselves—imprisoning people who were not criminals only to cast them out of prison, not because of humane sentiment, but because of the failure of the law to achieve its intended purpose. The ineffective cruelty of such legislation cried out for correction, and Beauchamp's proposal was a step in the right direction. "If we continue to oppose this bill," Burke warns, "we shall be found in a struggle against the nature of things."

The fullness of time, Burke maintains, will make clear the justice of this bill. Meanwhile, Burke can only lament the consequences of its defeat. Succumbing to the demands of his constituents, Burke had violated his own judgment, and so had relinquished any claim to leadership on the matter. As he concludes this third narration, Burke presents a short digression on the character of a certain Mr. Howard. Howard, it seems, had pursued the problem of debt legislation with constancy and foresight. For the moment, then, it is Mr. Howard and not Mr. Burke whom the audience must emulate. The lesson, in any case, is made clear: Howard's judgment was based and executed not on popular ignorance, but on individual virtue and knowledge born of experience. Howard's "plan," moreover, "is original; and it is as full of genius as it is of humanity. It was a voyage of discovery, a circumnavigation of charity. Already the benefit of his labor is felt more or less in every country; I hope he will anticipate his final reward by seeing all its effects fully realized in his own."

Narrative 4: Virtue and Tolerance

The fourth and final narration, however, once again places the orator at the center of the paradigm. Burke's role in the reform of Catholic penal laws reveals a character fully worthy of emulation. His actions, as in the first two sections, instantiate the principles established at the outset of the speech. But in this case, the issue is drawn more sharply and in more detail. The final narrative is far longer than any of the others, and it reduces itself to a story of the individual will confronting and overcoming the rage of popular unrest. At the same time, and consistent with the increased momentum of the text, the conflation of character and action, which indirectly permeates the whole work, now finds explicit statement. The Catholic problem, Burke asserts, "is a business closely related with the rest. They are all on one and the same principle. My little scheme of conduct, such as it is, is all arranged. I could do nothing but what I have done on this subject, without confounding the train of my ideas and disturbing the whole order of my life." He is nevertheless concerned to address the recent course of legislation aimed at Catholic relief. Knowing full well that his Bristol constituents hold him partly responsible, Burke cannot very well ignore the vexing issue of religious loyalties. But by situating his conduct within the pattern of reasoned action explained above, Burke manages to exculpate himself on consistent, if not convincing, terms.

Having announced this principle of unity, Burke turns to the specific issue in a way that typifies his whole train of thought. He undertakes his account of events by disengaging them from their immediate context, seeking instead to relocate the crisis within its larger historical and ethical context. From such a perspective, the proper standard of judgment makes its appearance amid the clutter of detail, and the audience is invited to judge the orator in terms of his fidelity to that standard.

Precedents to sectarian strife date back to the Reformation, Burke begins, but until the spirit of persecution is banished, the work of the Reformation remains incomplete. Protestants, seeking to dismantle "the vast structure of superstition and tyranny" of papal authority, often succeeded only in reversing the terms of hatred. Their notorious penal codes thereby became symbols of hypocrisy, and where, Burke says, "those laws were not bloody . . . they were worse; as they were slow, cruel outrages on our nature, and kept men alive only to insult in their persons every one of the rights and feelings of humanity." As Burke proceeds to examine the origin and progress of such codes, it becomes clear that their intolerance was rooted in a lack of perspective, an incapacity to chart prudently a course between extremes. Catholic action led to equally severe Protestant reaction, and the injuries of the moment destroyed all balance. It was not until the arrival of William, "our glorious deliverer," that reforms were effectively pursued. And they were secured, Burke is eager to stress, through steady commitment to natural principles of justice. The point, we may presume, is that William had to act in accordance with principles greater than fleeting prejudice. "Such is the effect of a tolerating spirit," Burke explains, "and so much is liberty served in every way, and by all persons, by a manly adherence to its own principles. Whilst freedom is true to itself, everything becomes subject to it, and its very adversaries are an instrument in its hands."

It was to rectify this historically driven chain of injustices that Sir George Saville introduced his bill. Saville's role, on Burke's account, was particularly noteworthy because it originated from a desire to preserve the true Protestant spirit and to protect Protestantism against its own excesses. In this sense, Saville displayed "his rooted hatred to all kinds of oppression, under any color, or upon any pretense whatsoever." Saville, in other words, understood that the difference between principle and extremism consisted in the capacity to judge events from an enlarged perspective.

Unhappily, popular opinion too often failed to achieve the same perspective. Although the bill repealed but one of the prejudicial statutes, it encountered a storm of public outrage. "No Popery" riots spread throughout London, and sectarian violence marked every stage as the anti-Catholic codes were dismantled. The public demanded that Commons uphold the codes. Burke, for his part, applied his energy against such pressure, freely acknowledging his resistance to its presence. In fact, he recounted, "I called forth every faculty that I possessed, and I directed it in every way in which I could possibly employ it. . . . If, therefore, the resolution of the House of Commons, refusing to commit this act of unmatched turpitude, be a crime, I am guilty among the foremost." But if Burke stood convicted in the verdict of transient opinion, he was vindicated by reflexive judgment. He steadfastly held his ground in principle and refused to desert the course of honor even against the powerful blasts of intolerance. And once again, time itself redeemed his stance, proving that true expediency arises from principle. Later events were to place England in grave peril from abroad, and the country was saved the catastrophe of internal subversion added to foreign threat only because Saville's act had secured the loyalty of the Catholic population. Such toleration as Burke could effect served honor and expediency. The resolution of the crisis at hand had demanded principles discerned from a more remote perspective. That perspective, in this case as in all others, defined the ground of political judgment. In exercising such judgment the representative gathered the particular and the general into a unified conception. The course of the whole speech, in fact, had been a journey toward this realization: "The diversified, but connected fabric of universal justice is well cramped and bolted together in all its parts; and depend upon it, I have never employed, and I never shall employ, any engine of power which may come into my hands to wrench it asunder. All shall stand, if I can help it, and all shall stand connected."

Conclusion

In his perceptive study of Burke's rhetorical art, Christopher Reid concludes that rhetoric, far from being the enemy of thought, is rather its "boon companion. It is the mode in which thought is energised and in which philosophy is translated into action."[9] Reid's observation reminds us of the dynamic quality of Burke's principles, of the speaker's insistence that ideas be mediated, indeed celebrated, within the spaces of public action. At the same time, Burke's Bristol address displays the struggle required to keep those principles vital, and so bears the marks and scars of a discourse at odds with its own audience. Still, out of that struggle, Burke provides a compelling if not altogether convincing case for the free exercise of political virtue.

All told, Burke's *Speech to the Electors of Bristol* establishes and enacts a paradigm for political judgment.[10] Almost all of its arguments bear upon the key problems in dealing with judgment—the coordination of spatial and temporal conceptions relevant to making political decisions. The essence of Burke's position is that the fluctuating and ambiguous subjects of political deliberation demand judgment disciplined by critical distance. The legislator must operate in a free space where reflective principles can mediate and shape the response to particular situations. In assuming this ground, the judging subject is not alienated from the particular, since distance in space creates a perspective from which an enlarged view of things can emerge. Indeed, lacking this perspective, political deliberation is not simply unprincipled, but ineffective; judgment can engage particulars successfully only when it comprehends them in terms of the general sweep of history. Consequently, Burke collapses the expedient into the honorable and defends the autonomy of judgment as a necessary control over the uncertain conditions of political action.

5

Staging Public Virtue in the
Impeachment of Warren Hastings

More so than any of his other causes, Burke's pursuit of Warren
Hastings was and remains most vulnerable to charges of grandstand-
ing, excess, and self-interest. There is, indeed, an obsessive quality
to Burke's character throughout the 1780s, and it is made evident in
his rhetorical practice. Volumes of Burke's printed works attest to
both the extraordinary moral fervor that elevated the prosecution
and the sheer excess that burdened it. Given the mass of detail—the
interminable speeches and extensive committee reports—the selec-
tion of any given text here is bound to be in some degree arbitrary. A
few of course stand out: Burke's speech on the Nabob of Arcot's
debts, for example, and his speech in support of Fox's East India
Bill. But for drama, for rhetorical contrivance and pageantry, surely
Burke's opening speech of impeachment before Lords and Commons
stands as his greatest moment. "There have been spectacles more
dazzling to the eye," Macauley wrote, "more gorgeous with jewelry
and cloth of gold, more attractive to grown-up children, than that
which was then exhibited at Westminster; but, perhaps, there never
was a spectacle so well calculated to strike a highly cultivated, a
reflecting, an imaginative mind."[1] Here, before the assembled powers
of the empire, Burke seemed finally to command the attention of
history.

In addition to its personal and political significance, the speech is
an exemplary instance of Burke's discourse of virtue. This, too, is a
discourse about relationships, about the coordinates of power and

the good, about the space of virtue and the possibilities of political action. So much the speech holds in common with those we have examined. It stands apart from the others, however, because of its staging, and while we are not used to thinking of virtue as something to be staged, it is precisely Burke's rhetorical achievement to put it on display and thus celebrate its power. This is rhetorical action on a grand scale, an interplay of warring values, an epic contest between good and evil that sweeps into itself speaker, audience, and empire.

Background

In the winter of 1785 Burke was disconsolate. For all his labors, his intricate maneuvering, and his strategic staging, the grand spectacle of his campaign against Warren Hastings was already showing signs of impending failure. Burke confided to his friend Philip Francis that "we bring before a bribed tribunal a prejudiced cause." All that remained, he wrote, "is to make a case strong in proof and in importance, and to draw inferences from it justifiable in logick, policy, and criminal justice. As to the rest," Burke concludes, "it is vain and idle."[2]

If Burke really believed the "rest" to be "vain and idle," then here is a remarkable confession indeed; more likely, as the following years were to suggest, Burke was merely and momentarily tired, for the campaign against Hastings was so long and so monstrously complex that it quite nearly exhausted the inexhaustible Burke. In the end, after the personal venom had been spent and all the arguments and evidence compiled, the goal remained fixed. "Speaking for myself," Burke writes, "my business is not to consider what will convict Mr. Hastings (a thing we all know to be impossible) but what will acquit and justify myself to those few persons and to those distant times, which may take a concern in these affairs and the actors in them."[3]

Burke had always been acutely sensitive to the judgment of history, so much so that he can easily—and plausibly—be faulted for speaking to it when more immediate issues demanded his attention. The decade of the 1780s, however, was to prove especially challenging to Burke's sense of historical identity. He had lost the prestigious Bristol seat for perfectly justifiable reasons; entering government as Paymaster of the Forces, he was summarily dismissed when the ill-fated Fox-North coalition self-destructed; Lord Rockingham, friend, confidant, and patron, died in 1782; and Pitt's assumption of power in 1784 seemed to usher in a new generation of political actors.

Threatened by an eclipse of his personal and political fortunes, Burke found in Hastings a cause worthy of his prodigious energies, and it detracts nothing from Burke's intentions to say that India's sorrow was his means to rejuvenation. In it he discovered a way to "acquit and justify" himself to posterity.

Of Hastings the man Burke knew little. As late as 1784, he wrote "I am no enemy of that man—he is nec odio nec beneficio mihi cognitus [known to me neither for good nor ill]." Burke was more certain, however, that under Hastings's rule India "is sacked and pillaged and I know he is the Government and I know a great deal more."[4] Burke indeed knew a great deal more than most about the career of Hastings, the East India Company, and British misrule in India. It was in any case a story of Byzantine complexity. Here we can only begin to sketch its progress and trace its role in English domestic politics.

Since its founding in Elizabethan England, the East India Company had grown by fits and starts into a formidable agency for English imperial interests. By the mid-eighteenth century, its peculiar combination of political and commercial power had become its most vulnerable trait. Even its leadership, however gratuitously, would complain that the "Company's orders were not to act offensively. . . . We don't want conquest and power; it is commercial interest only we look for."[5] Whether the East India Company wanted such power or not, they were by midcentury deeply committed to ensuring the English presence in India. In 1757 the battle of Plassey gave to the company control over Bengal and turned the surrounding nabobs into useful satellites; by 1761 it had vanquished a long-standing French threat. At the same time, serious questions regarding East Indian rule, as well as the standing enigma of a commercial power wielding political might, meant that it was not to be long before the state began investigating new possibilities for control and reform. Though certainly not the first to confront the problem, Burke soon emerged as its chief combatant.[6]

On 15 February 1788 Burke launched his campaign against Hastings, and he did it in grand style. In anticipation of the opening speech, the London Times reported that "The House of Peers now offers an object of the most solemn magnificence, that is at any time, or anywhere, presented to the attention of mankind."[7] Attention seems to have been on the minds of many: Burke's audience was said to have included a resplendent coterie of fifty-four barons; seventeen bishops; sixty-eight viscounts, earls, and marquises; twelve dukes; nine judges, and four princes of the blood. For one whose political fortunes were uncertain, who had spent so many years in opposition, and who had lost so many divisions, Burke must have drunk deeply the scene before him. "The expectation of Mr. Burke's opening the Charges of Impeachment," the *Times* noted, "drew a much more numerous assemblage to Westminster Hall, than had attended on any of the preceding days. At nine o'clock the carriages began to throng in great numbers—at eleven the galleries were nearly filled by Visitors."[8]

At two-thirty in the afternoon Burke sat down. The speech had lasted three hours. A witness for the *European Magazine and London Review* observed that Burke's oration was "grave and temperate; but was pathetic and affecting. Every expression and sentiment was appropriate; and though in the progress he led the ignorant to the most familiar acquaintance with the origin of the crimes and the evils of India, he astonished the most knowing with the new aspect which he gave to the whole."[9] All the planning, the contrivance and staging, had come together. Burke's pageant had given to his audiences an experience to remember.

Analysis of the Text

Virtue for Burke was explicable only as it was given structure, ordered by the concrete terms of motive and political action. This concern to establish proper order is therefore evident from the very first lines of the address. Assuring his august listeners that it is justice at work, and not merely the ambition of individuals, Burke strikes the first of many contrasts between his lawful conduct and the unwarranted actions of the accused. Far from renegade greed, Burke's motives are revealed as he acts under order of Parliament itself. Unlike his adversary, the speaker understands the moral imperatives embodied within the institution; he is its voice, not its arbitrary master. Burke makes the posture conspicuous by recurrently stressing his role as mere spokesman: the managers "have directed me to open the cause with a general view. . . . They have directed me to accompany this with another general view of the extent, the magnitude, the nature, the tendency, and the effect of the crimes. . . . They have also directed me to give an explanation . . . they wished me to add a few illustrative remarks."[10] By so submitting to the will of Parliament, Burke positions himself both in relation to its moral authority and Hastings's venality.

The source and object of his own authority comprise only part of Burke's rhetorical order. He is, after all, speaking to an immediate audience; and if he is in the long run acquitting himself to history, he nevertheless must confront those before him now. The gestures of companionship come early, and they provide the conventional functions of bringing together speaker and audience. But more than this, Burke's artful bow before Lords reaffirms his own identity as a public servant; his charge to them redirects our gaze from speaker to audience, from the obviousness of Burke's ambition to the solemnity of enlightened judgment. Hence the time-honored defacement of speaker before audience is deployed with cunning; the image of a man simply doing his duty is glorified by the enormity of the circumstances. Events have magnified the terms of moral action and have elevated everyone—except Hastings—to a position of supreme importance. "My Lords," Burke reminds his audience, "the business of this day is not the business of this man, it is not solely whether the prisoner at the bar be found innocent or guilty, but whether millions of mankind shall be made miserable or happy."

Burke's introductory lines signal in this way the early moments of a process that will drive his argument throughout. Its internal dynamic is synecdochic: parts stand for wholes, the lesser for the greater. This is the rhetoric of Burke's speech: what is before us is only the mark or signature of that which is not. In order for Burke to achieve this kind of rhetorical transference, he must elevate and magnify what is mundane and immediate. More than a mere trial, this is a grand inquest; more than a barrister, Burke is the spokesman of virtue itself. Hastings, as Burke will stress at great length, is no petty criminal, but the embodiment of all that is venal and corrupt in political life. And Lords, more than a jury, come to represent the agency for imperial good.

Burke's charge to the jury is, in effect, an epic gesture of trust. By its favor "the whole character of your future government in that distant empire is to be unalterably decided." How deeply portentous, how permanent are the consequences of that judgment, Burke is quick to make clear: "It will take its perpetual tenor, it will receive its final impression, from the stamp of this very hour." This habitual elevation of the specific to the general has the effect of conjoining individual and state; it is a means to reorder relationships violated by breaches in the public trust. When successful, the synecdoches broaden perspective and allow audiences to see what fits with what. Such a reordering, Burke makes clear, can shape moral perspectives as well. For Burke, the question of order is very much a matter of public virtue. As society cannot exist without order of a kind, the aims of civic action will be directed by this need. No more obvious an example could present itself than that suggested by the Hastings affair. Here the individual is projected into the state, the present into future, and the judgment into an act of historic significance. At stake, therefore, is not just the fate of India. Burke reasons that "the credit and honor of the British nation itself will be decided by this decision. We are to decide by this judgment, whether the crimes of individuals are to be turned into public guilt and national ignominy, or whether this nation will convert the very offenses which have thrown a transient shade upon its government into something that will reflect a permanent lustre upon the honor, justice, and humanity of this kingdom."

The means by which Hastings was brought to trial, the long and arduous march toward this moment, Burke thought a happy confirmation of English constitutional government. Others, not least the accused, saw it differently. But for Burke, the trial was evidence of the "individuating principle that makes England what it is." Venerable, rational, disinterested, the process ensured a democracy of virtue. "In this court," Burke announces, "no subject, in no part of the empire, can find a proportionable justice; here it is that we provide for that which is the substantial excellence of our Court,—I mean, the great circulation of responsibility by which . . . no man, in no circumstance, can escape the account which he owes to the laws of his country."

The process that Burke here celebrates is its own virtue. As it orders and directs "the circulation of responsibility," the Constitution sustains—demands—a powerful inclination toward human community. Burke's introductory remarks dramatize this maxim and apply it to trial, jury, and accused alike. Here as elsewhere, the speaker employs a principle to structure particulars, even as he points to specifics as evidence for the integrity of principle. It is a convenient mode of reasoning, to be sure, but it is exercised so often in Burke's discourse, and often so forcefully, that we are apt to miss its unifying function. Its success as a rhetorical resource depends on how well the speaker can align ideas and circumstances into compelling relationships. Certainly Burke's legacy is due in no small part to just this skill. For Burke's audience to see and consent to these images of moral order—his vision of public virtue—it must command his perspective; and it can only command his perspective if it consents to his ordering of the details. Burke, of course, is more than eager to assist: "It is by this tribunal that statesmen who abuse their power are accused by statesmen and tried by statesmen, not upon the niceties of narrow jurisprudence, but upon the enlarged and solid principles of state morality." As we might now expect, the passage does double duty; practically, it helps diminish the worrisome technical expertise of Hastings's counsel. More generally, it situates prosecutor and jury in a realm of enlightened judgment and public virtue.

Burke's charge to the jury does not complete his introduction. If anything, the entire speech is but an introduction to the grand and ultimately tragic story of Burke's campaign. Accordingly, he aims here to rationalize and justify the cause. The point is not so much to prosecute the individual as to promote the means by which Hastings was brought to justice. As with *Discontents*, *Speech on Taxation*, and *Speech to the Electors of Bristol*, Burke's address to Lords is highly reflective on its own mode of proceeding. It is not for that reason a meditation, but a thickly layered argument that serves its purposes on at least two levels. First, we should keep in mind that Burke's vigilance exceeded all those around him—so much so, in fact, as to invite suspicions of self-interest, even hysteria. It is not too surprising, therefore, to see in the speech a distinctive concern to legitimize itself. If the speech was to succeed, Burke had to impress upon his listeners not only Hastings's vice, but the prosecutor's virtue. The speech in this sense departs from the conventional forensic genre. Here the character of the accuser is as much contrived as that of the accused.

How Burke manages at once to indict Hastings and acquit himself is suggested by his narrative of events leading to this moment. He will recurrently identify himself within a complex of constitutional directives and, conversely, depict Hastings as abrogating these principles of community. Consequently, to question Burke's motives is to question English constitutional law; to ignore Hastings is to ignore its political and moral imperatives. Burke thus again deflects attention away from suspicions of private animosity, elevates his role to a purely public function, and redirects attention to Hastings as a public servant corrupted by personal avarice. This reordering is key to Burke's success and to our understanding of his rhetorical artistry.

The very structure of Burke's narrative highlights and promotes this posture of orderliness. Acting under directives from the managers, the speaker proceeds systematically to recount the intricate process leading to impeachment—the crimes committed, the charges, and the evidence gathered. The audience is thereby reminded of Burke's own reasoned mode of procedure, legitimized by convention and reflecting favorably on the speaker's own character. Careful to the point of being punctilious, the managers had acted with deliberation and always with precedent. They had acted, that is, in ways directly in contrast with the accused. Commons, Burke assures the House, "conducted themselves with singular care and caution. Without losing the spirit or zeal of a public prosecution," he continues, "they have comported themselves with such moderation, temper, and decorum as would not have ill-become the final judgment, if with them rested the final judgment, of this great cause." Moderate, tempered, decorous: these are the standards against which his antagonist is to be tried.

Obliged to act by the press of circumstances, Commons resolved to bring Hastings forward. Burke's account of these early proceedings depicts a House highly self-conscious of its duty and the dictates of protocol. All is caution, restraint, and "painful duty." Commons not only acted justly, Burke declares, but with such virtue as to set a precedent for ages to come: "We have chosen . . . such a crime, and such a criminal, and such a body of evidence, and such a mode of process, as would have recommended this course of justice to posterity." Without much in the way of precedent, Commons patiently heard "that insolent and unbecoming paper which lies upon the table"; they prudently "passed by everything offensive in that paper with a magnanimity that became them"; and in due course, "after a deliberation, not short of judicial, we proceeded with confidence to your bar." Innocence, Burke will note later, is plain, simple, direct—like Commons, perhaps he meant to suggest.

If the process had been exemplary of English justice, the crimes it revealed exemplified the opposite. Burke moves quickly from his reflections on constitutional restraint to a vivid portrayal of Hastings's rapacity. The effect is to rotate a series of juxtaposed values; here the speaker invites his audience to shift its gaze from the solemnity of virtue to the lurid image of embodied evil. So ordered, the audience sees in Hastings's crimes the moral counterpart to the actions of Parliament—that is, to itself. In both cases, Burke describes their respective acts as defining their essence; Parliament and Hastings are what they do. This mode of depiction allows Burke to hold before his audience artfully composed portraits of itself and its other. Burke must reveal Hastings as evil in action; he must induce Lords to see in rendering judgment a positive counterpart.

The crimes of Hastings, Burke stresses, are no ordinary transgressions. In Hastings they are laid deep in the contours of his character. By presenting Hastings in this way, Burke preempts any suggestion that Hastings may have merely erred as others might. The crimes, rather, were expressions of a certain type of character, "substantial," and they reveal the essential corruption that is Hastings. "We know," Burke explains, "as we are to be served by men, that the person who serves us must be tried as men, and with a very large allowance indeed to human frailty and human error." This extended effort to depict the nature of the crimes accurately is telling; it reminds us again of Burke's general concern for aligning relationships. By declaring what these crimes are not—incidental—he prepares his listeners for what they are in fact. Burke thus shifts the locale of Hastings's evil from the familiar scene of human action, the realms of politics and commerce, to a more alien, more violent and chaotic world where such evil, far from being incidental, defines the man himself.

No, Burke announces, Hastings is no ordinary man, and these are no ordinary crimes. And from such transgressions against human decency can be traced the animus of Hastings's character. "We charge this offender with no crimes," Burke says, "that have not arisen from passions which it is criminal to harbor,—with no offences that have not their root in avarice, rapacity, pride, insolence, ferocity, treachery, cruelty, malignity of temper." Here a literal litany of sins proclaim not only a set of actions, but the character of the actor. Hastings not only committed certain crimes, he did so out of an essentially criminal will. Burke's syntax—itself relentless, bordering on the excessive—serves his purposes well; like Hastings, it is furious, powerful, barely under control. And while brief, the passage signals a growing sense of outrage, where the posture of restraint is momentarily unsettled by the mere mention of Hastings's crimes. As if driven by the force of his own realization, Burke draws on this outrage to conclude the charges: Hastings is guilty of "nothing that does not argue a total extinction of moral principle, that does not manifest an inveterate blackness of heart, dyed in grain with malice, vitiated, corrupted, gangrened to the very core."

This "core," Hastings's malevolent essence: there is Burke's object, and his depiction is designed to get at it as quickly and dramatically as possible. If Burke is to expose its rottenness, if he is to implicate successfully not only the man but the very evil embodied in the governor-general, then the free agency of the accused must be established. Burke can thereby indict at once the individual and the system of values represented by the accused. For this reason, Burke continues, "If we do not plant his crimes in those vices which the breast of man is made to abhor, and the spirit of all laws, human and divine, to interdict, we desire no longer to be heard on this occasion." The bluff is obvious enough, but to a purpose; it highlights the elevated moral tone Burke is trying to sustain, and it affirms his insistence that extraordinary crimes are not to be apprehended under excessively constrained legalities. Conscious, no doubt, of the legal talent before him, Burke concludes by warning once again that Hastings's crimes were "crimes, not against form, but against those eternal laws of justice which are our rule and our birthright. His offences are, not in formal, technical language, but in reality, in substance and effect, *high* crimes and misdemeanors."

Burke carries forward this mode of description into his third category of review: the criminal himself. The move is patently strategic. By saving Hastings for last, Burke capitalizes on the accumulated effect of his preceding descriptions, and the indictment carries with it a familiar tone of outrage. The direction of Burke's attack can be anticipated as well. Where Hastings's crimes were shown to be "substantial" not incidental, so now Burke exposes the man in all his power, commanding in his very evil the status of an internationally important figure. "We have not chosen to bring before you," Burke explains, "a poor, puny, trembling delinquent . . . an obscure offender who, when his insignificance and weaknesses are weighed against the power of the prosecution, gives even to public justice something of the appearance of oppression." It is Hastings's stature, in fact, his prominence in the world of affairs, that warranted such proceedings in the first place. Burke dwells on the point to some effect. By stressing the inflated power of the accused, the speaker can hold before Parliament the image of something great grown monstrous, a character capable of such enormous crimes that he grants an equivalent greatness to those who would convict him. Burke accordingly announces that "we have brought before you the first man of India, in rank, authority, and station. We have brought before you the chief of the tribe, the head of the whole body of Eastern offenders, a captain general of iniquity, under whom all the fraud, all the peculation, all the tyranny in India, are embodied, disciplined, arrayed, and paid."

Burke's portrayal, if successful, suggests more even than a pillory of Hastings. To the degree that his character is made convincingly evil, the audience will view with suspicion any related activity in Hastings's past. The strategy, of course, is explicable as old-fashioned forensic assassination. Burke is making certain that Hastings is perceived as incapable of virtue; having established this perception, he can with confidence recount Commons' discovery of evidence. Hastings had been active, it turns out, in attempting to destroy access to sources and information; and some believed that Commons was acting merely to cover up its own role in the affairs of the East India Company. As a result, Burke is obliged yet again to protect and promote the integrity of his cause.

We have seen thus far how Burke responds to imagined or real suspicion. Elevating the terms of the contest, driving particular issues toward the upper reaches of significance, the speaker reenacts the dispute in a new language. Typically, Burke gives expression to the actions of Commons in ultimate terms. Thus he reminds his audience that when "you consider the late enormous power of the prisoner,—when you consider his criminal, indefatigable assiduity in the destruction of all recorded evidence . . . when you consider the distance of the scene of action,—I believe your Lordships, and I believe the world, will be astonished that so much, so clear, so solid, and so conclusive evidence of all kinds has been obtained against him." At this level nothing is routine, not even the conventional scrutiny of evidence before the bar. His eye on the future, conscious always of his place in history, Burke cannot allow questions regarding evidence to intercede in this grand display of justice: "God forbid the Commons should desire that anything should be received as proof from them which is not by nature adapted to prove the thing in question!" Within the confines of Burke's logic, the enormity of the occasion, the crimes, and the consequences reflect on English character. Any misuse of evidence, then, "would give the nation an evil example that would rebound back on themselves, and bring destruction upon their own heads, and on those of all their posterity."

Speaker, audience, accused, country: Burke's remorseless effort to magnify their historical portent is entirely in keeping with his celebration of political virtue. Burke understood virtue as it was displayed in the agon of history and played out in the great contests of public life. Virtue had to be seen to be truly meaningful, and it had to be held up as part of a grand spectacle of human activity. That is why so much in Burke's discourse is pitched in such ultimate terms—the point was not to exaggerate the claims of virtue, but to give it the most advantageous place among the competing habits of mankind. This movement upwards, always toward the greater, is characteristic of Burke's discourse of virtue, for virtue is made great by being realized in the general significance of particular events, people, and ideas.

Virtue is arrived at. It represents a cumulative process, and its discourse will reflect this movement. This is why in Burke the particular is so seldom allowed to remain still; he needs to open it up, to seize it, and to make it more meaningful than it ostensibly is. The result is a copious style, to be sure, capable at times of trying even the most dogged reader. More important, the discourse can be seen to embody the values it promotes, at least as it inscribes into the affairs of the moment marks of greater historical portent. When Burke therefore speaks of the application of municipal law to imperial problems—a matter of some concern to the prosecution—he must place the technical point within its full sweep of signification. "For the honor of this nation," Burke explains, "in vindication of this mysterious Providence, let it be known that no rule formed upon municipal maxims . . . will prevent the course of that imperial justice which you owe to the people that call to you from all parts of a great disjointed world." Sensitive always to the suspicions of history, Burke warns those before him that England, "an object, thank God, of envy to the rest of nations, its conduct in that high and elevated situation will undoubtedly be scrutinized with a severity as great as its power is invidious." Things greater than they seem, he argues, demand judgment of appropriate scope.

With his preliminary standards in place, positioned now to direct the reception of his narrative, Burke proceeds to explain the general circumstances of the Hastings affair. It is a story strange in place and meaning, and Burke is plainly concerned to tell it to advantage. He is, as we have seen repeatedly, intent on instructing his audience in the art of interpretation, of reading significance into the conduct of human activity—especially alien conduct. The narration is strategically presented on two levels as a way of securing this end. The audience is led to witness the factual unfolding of events in time, and it is encouraged to reflect on how those events are to be grasped fully and judged adequately. As a narrative, Burke's story imposes an evident order and sequence onto seemingly arbitrary events. This structuring into coherence serves Burke's purposes well. It draws attention to Burke's own ordered discourse, and hence juxtaposes the moral disorder of Hastings's legacy. Burke, in effect, structures the moral terms of his narrative through a process of identification, wherein the speaker personifies the virtues of reason—the logos— and Hastings embodies the evil of chaos. If there is an identity to Hastings's actions at all, Burke implies, it is in the form of insidious inversion, where the natural order of political meaning is at every turn distorted and where the principles of English virtue are undermined in the quest for self-gain. Burke in this way extends the series of moral contrasts to apply now not only to speaker and accused, but to English government over and against Indian misgovernment. And to the extent that his audience sees itself as representative of the former, he can solicit its sympathies with confidence.

Burke's narrative will be as successful as it is strange. He must, that is, dramatize Hastings's alien character and hold it up as a model of how not to rule. Burke therefore reminds his audience, perhaps unnecessarily, that all is not as it seems. To understand the nature of the situation, he implies, is to appreciate its basic peculiarity. Such an interpretation requires, in turn, a heightened sense of relationships, of order and of order violated. This much is essential to Burke's rhetorical aims; only by highlighting the virtue of ordered community and law can he impress upon his audience how far Hastings went in destroying its own commitments. Like the trial itself, Burke's narrative "has a relation to many things"; it "touches on many points in many places, which are wholly removed from the ordinary beaten orbit of English affairs."

The very strangeness of the circumstances, of course, places Burke in a privileged position. As the narrator, he commands a perspective not available to either the audience or the accused, and he is presumably best qualified to establish the terms of proper judgment. He wields the power of revelation, and if Lords are to exercise their judgment rightfully, they must then consent to Burke's telling. In this circumstance, Burke warns his listeners, "you are caught, as it were, into another world; you are to have the way pioneered before you. As the subject is new, it must be explained; as it is intricate as well as new, that explanation can be only comparatively short." Burke is therefore anxious that he be indulged for taxing their patience, "that your Lordships will not disdain to grant a few hours to what has cost the people of India upwards of thirty years of their innate, inveterate, hereditary patience to endure."

The patience that Burke seeks will be useful for another reason. As one who had defended the rights of charter vehemently a decade before, indeed as a career spokesman for imperial interests, he is in danger of being severely embarrassed. Burke cannot simply condemn the system that allowed Hastings to exist; he is too deeply implicated in the first place. He is not far into his account, then, before a strategic set of moves becomes evident. The empire was to Burke a form of community, expanded to be sure, but held together through enlarged sentiments and the proper ordering of its parts. Hastings's crime, Burke explains, lay not in being a part of that system, but in violating its terms. In Hastings, Burke discovered a metaphor of imperial disorder; under him the distinctive fusion of commercial and political interest driving the East India Company was made intolerable. As the object of Burke's portrayal, Hastings is associated with a series of similar inversions, where the agreed-upon standards of imperial community are perverted to suit private ends. Hastings is presented as the human embodiment of a system gone wrong; not its victim, but its champion, the terminal point of its corrupt career. The company itself was based on a principle, Burke explains, "not dreamt of in the theories of speculative politicians, and of which few examples in the least resembling it have been seen in the modern world, not at all in the ancient." Unlike other instances of imperial conquest, "here the course of affairs was reversed. The constitution of the Company began in commerce and ended in empire."

Burke's narrative, to the degree that it exposes this unnatural disposition of rule, stands as a lesson on how to read a complex, hidden text of political life. He directs his audience to uncover the ostensible and to see for itself; there, he suggests, can be found the real history of the company and its covert plan of conquest. Among other effects, this line of argument contains the added advantage of relieving speaker and audience of culpability in previously supporting the company. Because it was operating under cover, they cannot reasonably be held to account. "In fact," Burke argues, "the East India Company in Asia is a state in the disguise of a merchant. Its whole service is a system of public offices in the disguise of a counting house." Only after the efforts of Commons could the truth be told: "the whole external order and series of the service . . . is commercial; the principle, the inward, the real, is almost entirely political."

All that follows is a consequence of this basic position. Burke elaborates at great length on the distorted values and procedures that typified the company and piles example upon example to illustrate its threat to political virtue. Harms accumulate; evils expand and embrace an extraordinary range of experience; the sheer volume of detail overwhelms. As always, the consequences of Hastings's misrule comes back to undermine the prerogatives of Burke's own audience. Ultimately, Burke points out, the English in India were but fodder for company offices, and India itself "a commonwealth without a people" and "a kingdom of magistrates." It cannot be surprising, Burke concludes, that "by means of this peculiar circumstance it has not been difficult for Mr. Hastings to embody abuse, and to put himself at the head of a regular system of corruption."

As evidence of venality and crime accumulates, Burke is careful to keep before his audience a means to make sense of it all. This mode of presentation grants some relief to his audience, and it promotes the argument by attending to its status as credible history. Reflecting on his own method of proceeding, Burke legitimizes his claims by showing himself in control of the situation and material. It allows Burke to strengthen his posture at critical moments. As virtue's voice, Burke is mindful that advocates are apt to "indulge themselves in their narratives leading to the charges they intend to bring." But in such a place and under these circumstances, he reassures his audience, his case can be supported with the clearest of facts. Before passing to a final review of the Indian natives, Burke promises to buttress narrative portrayal with argumentative rigor: "I mean, by proof adapted to its nature; public opinion, by evidence of public opinion; by record, that to which record is applicable; by oral testimony, things to which oral testimony alone can be produced; and last of all, that which is a matter of historic proof, by historic evidence."

The remainder of Burke's address shifts attention away from the East India Company proper toward the Indian peoples. The description is detailed, richly textured, and composed in colorful strokes; it does not, however, allow the audience to lose perspective on the general themes of virtuous order thus far advanced. On this score, the climax occurs not in the oration's conclusion (for there is none), but soon after the narrative is reintroduced. Here the speaker pauses for a final time. Although the passage is not long, it represents the positive counterpart to his portrayal of Hastings and highlights again the moral alternatives before the audience. It is not enough, Burke implies, merely to indict Hastings; those who would indict the accused must appreciate the moral import of their own actions. Burke at this point offers a solution to the problem of Hastings; this solution he locates in the collective capacity for enlightened judgment represented in his audience. As a rhetorical gesture, this bow to his audience flatters even as it condemns the prisoner, and it encourages a view of the speaker as the guardian of justice.

This posture, this self-composed image of the statesman-as-exemplar, emerges into full view as the speech completes its course. Previously Burke had worked to drive apart English virtue and Hastings's character. Now he extends upon this opposition by uncovering the foundations of virtue and exposing by implied contrast the legacy of corruption. More than another in a series of such contrasts, the passage shows Burke most clearly in his role as reflective statesman. The posture allows him to elaborate for a final time on the imperatives of power; more than any other moment in the speech, this captures Burke's vision of imperial virtue. The litany of virtues is by now expected and gets framed to effect by its imaginative presentation:

If we undertake to govern the inhabitants of such a country, we must govern them upon their own principles and maxims, and not upon ours. We must not think to force them into the narrow circle of our ideas; we must extend ours to take in their system of opinions and rites, and the necessities which result from both: all change on their part is absolutely impracticable. We have more versatility of character and manners, and it is we who must conform. We know what the empire of opinion is in human nature . . . the strongest principle in the composition of the frame of the human mind; and more of the happiness and unhappiness of mankind resides in that inward principle than in all external circumstances put together.

For Burke, justification for the empire of opinion lay in the shared commitments of humanity, and Hastings's crime was to have violated its most basic laws. For this reason the trial was a grand exercise in public virtue, a celebration of virtue's triumph over venality. Hence the spectacle: it was display, and in displaying, the trial was itself designed as an act of virtue. That is why Burke seemed so unconcerned with its outcome or his particular fortunes as prosecutor. The trial alone was enough.

Conclusion

On the opening day of the prosection Fanny Burney settled herself in the gallery, readied for an afternoon of entertainment. Immediately, however, she was unnerved by the intensity and visual drama of the scene opening before her eyes. "I shuddered and drew involuntarily back," she recounted, "when, as the doors were flung open, I saw Mr. Burke, as head of the Committee, make his solemn entry. He held a scroll in his hand, and walked alone, his brow knit with corroding care and deep laboring thought." Seeing him thus, Burney noted, made her "grieve to behold him the cruel prosecutor (such to me he appeared) of an injured and innocent man!"[11]

Burney, of course, was not alone in resenting Burke's self-appointed role as chief prosecutor for the empire. Well into the twentieth century, in fact, Burke continued to be attacked for staging Hastings's crimes as he did. Thus Mervyn Davies could write a century and a half later that "as a tour de force [Burke's speech] was truly magnificent and filled his hearers with amazement at the prodigality of his genius," and at the same time insist that "every time Burke opened his mouth he did more harm than good to his cause."[12] If we judge Burke by the standards of immediate success or votes tallied, of course, we may be inclined to agree. But as with the *Speech on Conciliation*, such standards may be entirely beside the point. Burke was well aware of the odds, and if we remember his comment to Philip Francis—that "my business is not to consider what will convict Mr. Hastings . . . but what will acquit and justify myself to those few persons and to those distant times"—then we must reconceive the meaning and legacy of his discourse.

Of all Burke's campaigns, his fight for American interests, for economic reform, for Irish relief, for the French contagion, he thought the greatest to be the impeachment of Warren Hastings. Certainly it demanded the most from him; for a decade he labored— obsessively, a little ridiculously perhaps—to move an empire against one of its own. In the end, of course, he "failed"; Hastings was acquitted in April 1790 on all counts. But though Burke had in one sense failed—indeed on a prodigious scale—in another sense he had given to posterity what he had so long given to party. From beginning to end, his cause was held to be more important than its outcome, and there was for Burke no more important aim than to acquit himself in the service of that cause.

6

Political Virtue as Rhetorical Action in the *Letter to a Noble Lord*

Samuel Johnson once remarked, "what I envy Burke for, is his being constantly the same. He is never what we call hum drum; never unwilling to begin to talk, nor in haste to leave off."[1] However sardonically, Johnson captured what is central to the legacy of Burke, his relentless enthusiasm for talking politics. In an age famous for its conversationalists, Burke stands out as Johnson's only rival; as an orator, he spanned the political controversy of three decades. From this career there emerged a consistency of perspective and a body of political thought that has yet to lose its saliency. Burke's legacy, however, cannot be located at the level of his political principles only; this was, after all, the century of Bolingbroke, Montesquieu, and Hume. Nor can it be attributed to his oratory. The stage was crowded with such accomplished orators as Chatham, Grenville, Pitt the Younger, and Charles James Fox. Burke, rather, stands alone among these figures because he alone chose to negotiate political principle solely through the conventional genres of rhetoric. It is this fusion of an ancient and often antagonistic split between philosophy and rhetoric that constitutes Burke's achievement, and which in turn occupies the attention of this essay. How Burke manages this unity may be seen by examining not his oratory as such, but a written tract, the *Letter to a Noble Lord*.

The preceding studies in Burke's discourse of virtue indicate that Burke never forgot—was never allowed to forget—that virtue could only be a momentary achievement. As an orator, a pamphlet polemicist, and parliamentarian, he knew too that virtue was symbolically charged; it was in that sense a rhetorical construction and, hence, liable to the shifting contingencies of community and time. Now, in the final years of his life, he struggled still to reconstruct an image of virtue for himself and his country; both, he felt, were under siege. It should not be at all surprising that he turned to a rhetorical medium as a way of recapturing what he felt to be slipping away.

The interpretation I present and the conclusions offered are based upon a close and detailed reading of the text. Upon this basis, I investigate the ways in which Burke's political thought—his commitment to virtue—is configured into a rationale for public action. The *Letter to a Noble Lord* conducts this movement by empowering principle with motive and circumstance; aside from rewarding textual analysis of this kind, it thus provides an example of how theoretical precepts may be activated within the constraints of individual will and human community.

The significance of Burke's letter is twofold. It is, taken alone, a rewarding study in textual dynamics. My reading of the *Letter to a Noble Lord* is accordingly designed to illustrate its internal action and to promote this approach to the criticism of rhetorical texts. Such a reading is meant to establish the more general significance of the letter; it is a study in the collaboration of philosophy and rhetoric as motives to actions. This collaboration is achieved by the assertion of virtuous character into the sweep of historical change; thus the letter dramatizes the centrality of the individual and gives moral sanction to the arts of inducement. Here is an example in which the private sphere of contemplative knowledge is fused with the public sphere of political action. The unity of these spheres in the letter is evidence that in the affairs of the world, philosophical principle and rhetorical action need not be antagonistic. The product is an unusually poignant comment on the nature of virtue as an attribute of both the individual and the community. In this sense, it caps our series of readings by drawing together the many senses of virtue thus far discussed.

Although it delays somewhat our entrance into the *Letter to a Noble Lord* proper, the following review brings into focus the complexity of Burke's legacy and the problems he has posed to generations of scholars. At the heart of the matter is a question of attribution; was Burke a philosopher, driven ultimately by the pursuit of truth, or was he a rhetorician, motivated by self-interest and constrained only by the expedient? My analysis of the letter argues that neither appropriation is satisfactory; that, indeed, Burke's legacy is best understood as he negotiates his way between philosophy's private and rhetoric's public realms.

Burke's reputation in the nineteenth century was for the most part favorable. Vindicated by the outrages of the French Revolution, Burke indeed fared better in the nineteenth century than in his own. By century's end, Burke had been fully appropriated by utilitarian thinkers and Whig historians. It was Burke's zeal for economic reform, religious toleration, and social welfare that appealed most to the utilitarian mind; and if it was a mind forgetful of Burke's stand on the electoral base, it was always ready to exploit the eloquent attacks on penal codes and fiscal corruption. The historians and biographers who early sought to celebrate Burke's contributions were of just this stamp. John Morley, John MacCunn, Sir Leslie Stephens, and others gave great weight to Burke's appeals to expedience and the values of community. Burke's genius, they wrote, lay in his prudence, his empirical and relentlessly practical frame of mind. Thus W. E. H. Lecky wrote in his prodigious *History of England in the Eighteenth Century* that "it was the first principle of Burke and the school of Whigs politicians who took their politics from his writings, that government rests wholly on expedience, that its end is the good of the community, and that it must be judged exclusively by the degree in which it fulfils this end."[2]

Against a twentieth-century backdrop of conservative and cold war intellectualism, a natural law interpretation of Burke's thought quickly gained prominence. Far from operating under a utilitarian calculus, its proponents argued, Burke was a firm believer in the dictates of a universal, immutable, and natural law. As such, his politics could be arraigned under a series of principles, themselves generated from the timeless truths of God. Burke's writings were, according to this interpretation, deeply indebted to certain classical and Thomistic conventions.

Hence the weight of the natural law interpretation falls clearly upon Burke's philosophy. Politics serves largely as an illustration of his more general principles. There is, of course, much to support such an interpretation. Burke was an object of much complaint during his own life for precisely this reason: he confused the political stage with the closet of philosophy. But within the natural law interpretation of Burke, such a fact would be irrelevant. Of greater importance is the philosophical foundation upon which his politics rests. Thus Father Canavan, an especially rigorous student of Burke's political reason, writes it is "plain that Burke stated and used a full-blown theory of natural law, of whose metaphysical implications he was by no means unaware."[3]

Although the natural law interpretation of Burke's thought has remained dominant, it has not remained unchallenged. What the early utilitarians recognized in Burke could not be ignored by even the most staunch natural law theorist: his instinctive distrust of theory, abstract reasoning, and speculation. Burke's writings are shot through with a brand of skeptical empiricism not easily reconciled by adherents of natural law. Largely as a result of this failure to account for Burke's evident pragmatism, recent students of Burke's thought have sought to integrate the best of both utilitarian and natural law traditions. The rapprochement has been effected by emphasizing the pliability of Burke's principles and by insisting upon Burke's location within public life. Here situated, Burke's thought becomes a complex of moral standards and political needs. Less antagonistic than previously suggested, the relationship between principle and expedience is now taken to be necessary and positive. In *The Moral Basis of Burke's Political Thoughts*, Professor Parkin represents the best of this reinterpretation. "While Burke's thought is by design a response to immediate contingencies," Parkin writes, "it is in no sense an uncontrolled or arbitrary response, but always, in his own eyes, under the guidance of some moral principles, which certainly, to be real, must be reinterpreted, rediscovered, and reaffirmed in an infinity of specific and unique situations, but which represent themselves unchanging truths of human life and community."[4]

Although the contested interpretations of Burke's thought have been largely resolved, two significant problems remain. The first has to do with the very assumptions upon which a philosophical interpretation is or ought to be founded. The three schools of interpretive thought here represented—utilitarian, natural law, and those who would reconcile both—all conduct their enquiry at the level of content only. Whatever the competing perspectives, historians and theorists have categorically ignored the formal properties of Burke's thought, isolating the substance of his writings as if it could be made independent of rhetorical structure and meaning. As a result, whatever reconciliation that has been achieved remains problematic. Looking for and finding the stuff of political theory only, students of Burke have routinely failed to understand what Burke himself insisted upon: negotiating political ideas between the extremes of principle and expedience required a rhetoric of great complexity. Only Burke may be said to have left a legacy in which theoretical insight is joined to local circumstance as content is to form. For this reason, the study of Burke at the level of substance only cannot be satisfactory.

A second tradition shaping our understanding of Burke is a virtual counterpart to the first. Within this tradition Burke has been configured as a spokesman of uncommon artistry, indeed as the exemplary figure of eighteenth-century oratory. American critics, particularly those operating within the disciplines of speech and English, have done much to rehabilitate Burke's once quixotic reputation. No longer thought of as "dinner bell Burke" or as the slightly hysterical defender of the ancien régime, Burke is now fixed within a canonical literature.[5]

Burke, however, was not always thus placed, and currently there is little consensus on the precise nature of his art. For every critic inclined to applaud Burke's rhetorical skills, there are others who understand Burke's art as, above all, motivated, driven by material interests and ideological justification.[6] Best exemplified by the work of Namier, this perspective on Burke's rhetoric has attained wide support among historians; it has also qualified the enthusiastic claims of those who would make of Burke a detached and selfless statesman. Burke is taken as a propagandist for his party, albeit an unusually eloquent one. Encouraged by the claims of Namierite scholarship, historians have decentered Burke from the political stage and have seen in his rhetoric a man obsessed by his own righteousness and the conspiratorial desires of his enemies. In this way, O'Gorman writes, "as in so much else, Burke was echoing Rockingham's sentiments, not prompting them. In a very real sense, Edmund Burke was his master's voice."[7] Burke's rhetorical achievement, then, was to mask the motives of his party effectively through an aggressive appeal to principles and natural law. He was, at best, a party spokesman, at worst a frustrated and servile politician.

The conventional treatment of Burke as a rhetorician is then a complex of insight and shortcomings. We have seen that its failure has been to drive apart what in Burke is essentially unified. This too has been the failure of those who would locate Burke within certain theoretical traditions. To reestablish the unity of Burke's rhetorical art is one aim of this study; another is to discover the conceptual forces that sustain that unity. A new perspective on Burke's legacy will require a fresh approach to his art, one that takes seriously the discursive formation of ideas within identifiable contexts. Such an approach will ask not only what Burke said, but how he said it, and it will resist assigning meaning independent of structure and image.

The *Letter to a Noble Lord*

Approaching the end of a long and often harried life, Burke wrote to a friend that "my apology is that for the last years of my public service, I have been most painfully and disagreeably employed in bringing to a conclusion that principle act which is to be the glory or the shame of my whole public life."[8] We have no way of knowing exactly what "that principle act" is—whether he refers to the French Revolution or to his spirited campaign against its influence. In a sense we cannot separate the two, nor, I suspect, could the aging Burke. During his final years Burke's private ambitions and public affairs ignited a rhetoric of great force and complexity. Nowhere is this as evident as in the *Letter to a Noble Lord*.

Burke's *Letter* is not among his most famous works, but it is among his most significant. The pamphlet contains many of the traits a reader of Burke may expect: it is vehement, at times furious, at other moments calculated to suggest restrained reason.[9] Although critics and historians of public address have accorded the text little attention, its reputation as a strange but compelling tract is secure. The *Letter* has been judged "the most splendid repartee in the English language," by John Morley; others have thought it "the most elaborately wrought, the most gorgeous, of all his works" and "one of the great masterpieces of satirical and ironical repartee." Although F. L. Lucas believed that one now "Would no more write a pamphlet so rhetorically than he would compose a leading article in rhyme, or sing in the House of Commons," most students of Burke agree that the *Letter* is remarkable, "not only because it goes home to the quick, but because it smothers the spitefulness of its assailant in a flood of eloquence and wisdom."[10]

As a public tract, the *Letter to a Noble Lord* appeals to a universal audience of vicarious readers; as a private form it may evince an integrity not easily projected into the public realm. Burke's exploitation of the form is striking; the *Letter* reveals him pushing the medium to its limits and exercising its ambivalent status to render the public private and the private public. The epistolary form, by nature protean, accords Burke the opportunity to range across a spectrum of themes, to invoke a variety of styles of voices, and to transcend the limits of conventional rhetorical genres.[11] As the following review of the *Letter*'s immediate circumstances suggests, the epistolary form is ideally suited to Burke's ends, for all is action within and without. The *Letter*, in any case, resists reduction to argumentative structure or to the sheer analysis of style. It works, rather, by evoking a series of moral commonplaces. Clustered under the image of the "new man," these commonplaces are familiar in apologiac rhetoric as attributes of the individual. Burke invokes these commonplaces as a way of confronting the more general threat of French influence over English sympathies. Burke thus aims at the reclamation of a past under a siege by French revisionists and a public no longer certain of its monarchical loyalties.

Burke brings to the *Letter to a Noble Lord* and to the circumstances that gave rise to it a lifelong commitment to the sanctity of English history, the Constitution, and to the dictates of natural law. As transcendent principles, however, these constructs are never allowed to rest separate from or above human affairs. Burke employs them, rather, as guides for acting wisely. As the *Letter* unfolds, we are led to witness this movement from principle to action. This movement is organized on the basis of Burke's vindication, wherein the author comes to symbolize England herself. The *Letter* thus relocates its inducement to action from a private quarrel to a defense of the venerable principles of English government. Because the *Letter* achieves this relocation as it unfolds, we are obliged to follow its movement *in seriatim*. We are then in a position to see that, for Burke, principle is vital only to the extent that it is generated from the constraints of individual will and human community. A brief description of these constraints follows as a way into the text itself.

Personal and Political Background to the Letter

At no time in his life was Burke ever completely a man at home. Irish by birth, he suffered, indeed seemed at times to invite, the typical prejudices of eighteenth-century London. Born of a Roman Catholic mother and married to a woman of like faith, Burke struggled as well against widespread antipapist sentiment. He arrived in London at age twenty-one to pursue a legal education at the behest of his father; he seems to have had no intention of doing so and embarked upon a literary and investment career. These facts, though brief, tell us much. Burke was taken as something of an opportunist, a *novus homo* not always to be trusted. Although his rise in London social and intellectual circles was rapid, evidence suggests that he never shed this "new man" complex. In fact, the *Letter to a Noble Lord* tells us as much; it is shot through with a lifetime's worth of suspicion and bitterness. In government for only a brief period under the Rockingham administration, Burke learned to celebrate his fate as a leader in opposition politics; he fought as many important battles with as little success as anyone in parliamentary history. Never terribly popular in Commons, at times vilified in the press, Burke developed a rather thick skin as a matter of survival. At moments, however, he wavered, and we know that at least once he fell. Politics, however, continued to consume Burke's interests; no surprise, then, that toward the end of his career Burke's discourse often suggests that despair of a man haunted to his grave by enemies and all but forgotten by his friends.[12] The *Letter*, we shall find, is infused with these impulses, exposing now a public figure driven to personal defense, now again a man reasserting himself into a public of his own making.

Burke retired in 1794, exhausted from his interminable battles against Hastings and the spread of French revolutionary ideas. His reputation grew more favorable out of Commons than within. The *Reflections on the Revolution in France* (1790), the greatest of his public letters, was greeted with popular, if often controversial acclaim. Burke was not, to say the least, inclined to curry popular favor, but we must note this search for a new and uncertain public. Given his reputation historically, we are apt to forget his immediate audiences, and that like all masters of the art, he looked to them for vindication and support. In the quiet of his Beaconsfield estate, Burke found opportunity to substitute the parliamentary oration with the public letter. He thereby appealed to a far greater audience than could be found before a drowsy and often nearly empty House. But the world was different after the events of 1789, and so was Burke's discourse. Even as his obsession with the revolution kept him within the familiar constraints of the public realm, his rhetoric buried formal expectations under the weight of its own rage. It is just this rage, moreover, which gives the *Letter to a Noble Lord* its critical significance, in that it mirrors the energy and uncertainty of its audience. Here is a public caught between a new order and the old, at once repulsed by the carnage of the French Revolution and the arrogance of a dying aristocracy.[13] To a great extent, the scope and volatility of Burke's audience keeps the *Letter* from being mere invective; much more than that, it embodies the turbulent search for moral certainty at the heart of the late eighteenth-century English public. It is this public alone, in the end, which could invest Burke's arguments from principle with the force of social need.

Burke's Rhetorical Problem

The *Letter to a Noble Lord* was published as a pamphlet in response to an attack upon Burke in the House of Lords.[14] Ostensibly addressed to his friend Lord Fitzwilliam, it reached a wide and largely approving audience, answering insult with a complex synthesis of defense and counterattack. At its manifest level, the *Letter* is aimed at two young noblemen, the Duke of Bedford and the Earl of Lauderdale. Lauderdale, and especially Bedford, had taken objection to Burke's newly granted pension and had denounced him publicly for violating his own principles of economy and reform. By accepting the pension from the Crown, they claimed, Burke had compromised his earlier efforts to trim the civil list and patronage from the court. The grant, moreover, had been negotiated by William Pitt, then prime minister, and so engineered that it circumvented discussion in Parliament. Not only had Burke defied this traditional and democratic channel, but in accepting the pension had revealed his true colors as a minion to the Crown.

Beneath this apparent motive, however, there rested a greater design. For all its excesses, the French Revolution continued to inflame republican enthusiasm in England, even in quarters as unlikely and as staid as the House of Lords. Bedford and Lauderdale were proving themselves particularly susceptible to revolutionary doctrines and now exploited the pension issue as an opportunity to denounce the author of the *Reflections on the Revolution in France*. Burke was of course quite familiar with public attacks, and he had long defended his stance by recourse to tradition and constitutional precedent. Especially since 1789, he had appealed to the venerable balance of Crown, Church, and Parliament as bulwarks against the leveling force of French revolt. But here was a different matter, paradoxical and rhetorically difficult. How should Burke respond to an attack issued from the very political and social order he had written the *Reflections* to defend? As we shall learn, the *Letter to a Noble Lord* provides a remarkable example of how to make the most of an apparent dilemma. As we track its progression, we must follow the *Letter* as it unfolds, and coax from it an identifiable set of principles, suspended for a time, and finally resolved into the fabric of Burke's argument. As its seemingly chaotic structure fragments and recombines, the *Letter* subtly induces a process of mutation and transcendence, wherein private character vindicates public action and apologia ripens into deliberation. Constructed along a series of antithetical themes, the *Letter* ultimately reverses the moral orders of the attacker and the attacked. In this conflation of character and circumstance, form and function, the ad hominem argument is elevated from a fallacy of expedience to an issue of principle. And as he makes his way from a subordinate toward a superordinate role, Burke cuts across traditional genres to act as political adviser, prosecutor of social evil, and celebrant for the venerable principles of the ancien régime.

Upon first reading, the *Letter to a Noble Lord* does not appear to command an order at all. Burke's private life and public action clash with Bedford's ancestry and motives, and spatial and temporal referents thread in and out of the text with elusive regularity. Unless we choose to believe that its author had simply lost command of his art, we may suspect that the text functions in ways not readily apparent, that in fact its lack of obvious design is itself strategic.[15] Upon closer examination we discover a certain method to its structural madness. Playing freely within the epistolary form, Burke is able to juxtapose and extend upon principles with great liberty, able finally to effect a complete identification of private character with public action. The disorder then is dangerously obvious, and the reader must resist either imposing conventional order or abandoning the *Letter* as an unfortunate polemic. Instead, we are rewarded by realizing that although it is ostensibly a response to an attack upon the pension, the *Letter* goads us into losing sight of the particular and into considering issues of far greater significance.

Introduction to the Letter

Even as we are introduced to the *Letter to a Noble Lord,* conventional form gives way to a rapidly surfacing fury. Burke's initial posture is ironic and tinged with good humor; it is the stance of a man comfortable with his station. The posture, however, cannot be sustained in the face of public insult, and Burke's descent into pathos suggests the impotence of the marginal man. Burke initially thanks Bedford and Lauderdale for their attack, if only because it has prompted the likes of Lord Grenville to his defense. Burke writes, "Retired as I am from the world, and from all its affairs and all its pleasures, I confess it does kindle in my nearly extinguished feelings a very vivid satisfaction to be so attacked and so defended."[16] Immediately, however, Burke's ironic generosity vanishes, and as he reflects upon his antagonists, we move from private insult to public threat. The young noblemen become much more than young noblemen, and Burke's victimage much more than personal harm. With virtually no transition, Burke is led to observe that the "moral scheme of France furnishes the only pattern ever known which they who admire will instantly resemble." Such are Bedford and Lauderdale. As for Burke: "In my wretched condition, though hardly to be classed with the living, I am not safe from them. They have tigers to fall upon animated strength; they have hyenas to prey upon carcasses." This dramatic movement between public and private impulses sets the direction for much of the *Letter* and indicates something of its internal dynamic. But less apparent is the way in which Burke identifies his attackers with the French contagion and associates his own prospects with "the fate of all the human race." Hyperbole and satire roil with such relentless energy that again we lose sight of the original issues. Does Burke refer to his youthful antagonists or to the Jacobins threatening English liberties and order? "Their turpitude purveys to their malice," Burke continues, "and they unplumb the dead for bullets to assassinate the living. If all revolutionists were not proof against all caution, I should recommend it to their consideration, that no persons were ever known in history, either sacred or profane, to vex the sepulchre, and by their sorceries to call up the prophetic dead, with any other event than the prediction of their own disastrous fate.—Leave me, oh, leave me to repose!"

Caught somewhere between his private and public worlds, Burke's apologia, like his life, is ambivalent indeed. We sense in the early stages of the *Letter to a Noble Lord* Burke's desire for vindication, but it is vindication of a special sort. Its success will require the proper alignment of character to circumstance, and from it will emerge exemplary conditions of public action and judgment. To effect this alignment Burke will construct a series of synecdochic relationships, wherein Bedford comes to stand for England's peril and Burke himself for England's salvation. Within the logic of this structure, Bedford's sins are delusion and torpor. Burke, conversely, commands insight and the will to act in the presence of danger. But to act is to require a public, and it is only through a vindication of his character that Burke can move from the margins of his political world.

The attack itself—on the legitimacy of the pension—seems now rather beside the point, and yet, Burke cannot simply ignore the offense. After decades spent defending the traditional bases of constitutional monarchy, a challenge from its privileged orders must be met. Burke had, after thirty years of public disputation, rugged sensibilities. The real problem was that the attack issued from the House of Lords. In effect the confrontation placed Burke in a double bind: if he allowed the challenge to go unanswered he suffered personal offense and diminishment of his character. Should he attack the Lords, he risked vilifying a venerable institution. Burke of course was alive to the dilemma: "Loose libels ought to be passed by in silence and contempt. By me they have been so always. I knew, that, as long as I remained in public, I should live down the calumnies of malice and the judgements of ignorance." And, in fact, Burke continues, the "libels of the present day are just of the same stuff as the libels of the past." But, he concludes, "they derive an importance from the rank of the persons they come from, and the gravity of the place where they were uttered."

Narrative: Historical Vindication of Self and Society

How Burke negotiates his way out of this perplexity is revealed in the body of the *Letter to a Noble Lord.* Here autobiography and political history are combined with such force as to tear away Bedford's symbolic attachment to the existing structure. Driving apart character from system, Burke secures his own ascendence into a redeemed moral and political order. The narratives that conduct this transformation derive their rhetorical force from an amplification for which Burke is notorious: invective layers upon invective, image upon image, hyperbole upon hyperbole. The sheer weight of the argument demands that its form be given the widest possible latitude, and for this the public letter is a most appropriate medium.

As Burke turns now to the specific charges, we are in a better position to see his argument at work. Refuting Bedford, he refutes what Bedford stands for; and vindicating himself, Burke vindicates the English past. In this way the particular motives and local interests are fused with general principles into a rationale for public action. Thus the first narrative locates Burke historically and reveals him to have acted with principle and constancy. Bedford had alleged that Burke, in accepting the pension, was departing from such principle; Burke in turn recovers the past to prove the charge false. But the manner in which Burke vindicates himself is as important as the factual account. As he details his action during the economic crisis of 1780–82, Burke distinguishes himself from his detractors then and now, and he does so by invoking principles of judgment and action. There is rich ambiguity, therefore, in Burke's indictment: "I knew that there is a manifest, marked distinction, which ill men with ill designs, or weak men incapable of any design, will constantly be confounding,—that is, a marked distinction between change and reformation." The referent here is strategically uncertain, but we know that Burke's antagonists—all of them, in the past as well as the present—operate from the same false judgment. And we know that Burke had acted to protect England against such false judgment: in the past against those who resisted moderate economic reform; in the present against those who would threaten social order in the name of change.

The transition from time past to time present indicates more than simple narrative development. Burke makes proxemic the threat of false judgment and dangerous action, and he locates the threat in principles shared by Bedford and the revolutionaries alike. Here Burke is emphatic; theirs is a principle of false action and false order, insidious because confused. Hence the imagery and intensity of the following passage reflect Burke's own fears, and its syntax mimes the frantic disorder of his foes:

The consequences are before us,—not in remote history, not in future prognostication: they are about us, they are upon us. They shake the public security; they menace private enjoyment. They dwarf the growth of the young; they break the quiet of the old. If we travel, they stop our way. They infest us in town, they pursue us to the country. Our business is interrupted, our repose is troubled, our pleasures are saddened, our very studies are poisoned and perverted, and knowledge is rendered worse than ignorance, by the enormous evils of the dreadful innovation. The Revolution harpies of France, sprung from Night and Hell, or from that chaotic Anarchy which generates equivocally "all monstrous, all prodigious things," cuckoo-like, adultrously lay their eggs, and brood over, and hatch them in the nest of every neighboring state. These obscene harpies, who deck themselves in I know not what divine attributes, but who in reality are foul and ravenous birds of prey, (both mothers and daughters,) flutter over our heads, and souse down upon our tables, and leave nothing unrent, unrifled, unravaged, or unpolluted with the slime of their filthy offal.

Against such circumstances, character can be the only recourse. And this is precisely the achievement of the *Letter to a Noble Lord:* forever driving apart himself from his attackers, Burke dramatically holds up for inspection his own character as well as Bedford's. Vindicated by history, Burke emerges as the rightful defender of the realm. He achieves this role, however, without calling into question Bedford's claim to privilege or the order from which he speaks. Indeed it is just because of his character that Burke can dispense with Bedford and still celebrate the English system. Burke's marginality now becomes proof of character, and if we note the bitterness, we must note as well an irony full of celebration: "I was not, like his Grace of Bedford, swaddled and rocked and dandled into a legislator: '*Nitor in adversum*' is the motto for a man like me." Far from being a minion to the Crown, Burke continues, "[a]t every step of progress in my life, (for in every step was I traversed and opposed,) and at every turnpike I met, I was obliged to show my passport, and again and again to prove my sole title to the honor of being useful to my country."

As the tenor of Burke's apologia fades against this contrast in merit, the argument itself shifts structural focus. The narrative has worked to isolate Burke's relationship not only to his foes, but also to the system from which they pretend to draw strength. Burke will exploit this relationship with great effect later, but for now he is content to set up the initial stages of an ironic twist: "I have supported with very great zeal, and I am told with some degree of success, those opinions, or, if his Grace likes another expression better, those old prejudices, which buoy up the ponderous mass of his nobility, wealth, and titles." The ambivalence of his own status is thereby relocated in that of his opposition: representatives of the aristocracy, and not the aristocracy itself, are implicated in Burke's attack. He has, in effect, redefined the conditions of his argument.

From Burke's notorious arsenal of metaphors, perhaps none is as telling here as the whale image. With it Burke expands upon the "ponderous mass" of Bedford's House to render it faintly obscene. The likes of Bedford are not true representatives of their order but a burden to it. The paradox of Bedford's attack is thus cast back with great force; Bedford is "the leviathan among all the creatures of the crown. He tumbles about his unwieldy bulk, he plays and frolics in the ocean of the royal bounty." Burke, conversely, earned his small reward for a lifetime of service and merit. Inversion of the moral orders is nearing completion. "Huge as he is," Burke concludes, "and whilst 'he lies floating many a rood,' he is still a creature. His ribs, his fin, his whalebone, his blubber, the very spiracles through which he spouts a torrent of brine against his origin, and covers me all over with the spray, everything of him and about him is from the throne. Is it for him to question the dispensation of the royal favor?"

Burke's argument now pivots into a second narrative account of the two orders—one that grants reward on the basis of merit, the other virtue of lineage. As he pursues the contrast, Burke wrenches Bedford from his false source of power; again he does so by locating Bedford historically, and within this context exercises a perspective not available to the young nobleman. Full of portent and innocence Burke asks "Why will his Grace, by attacking me, force me reluctantly to compare my little merit with that which obtained from the crown those prodigies of profuse donation by which he tramples upon the mediocrity of humble and laborious individuals?" We sense, of course, that Burke is anything but reluctant to draw the contrast. He is taking on Bedford at his own ancestral game, and as Burke exposes the origins of the Bedford House, we find a name that did not so much earn its keep as scavenge it.

The historical narrative that Burke now undertakes is decisive. At one level the account stigmatizes Bedford by aligning him with the corrupt Tudor regime; at another the narrative shows Burke enacting history, that is, exercising a form of judgment enriched by the past and finally vindicated by its lessons. Together, these two levels of the narrative drive apart the disputants and elevate Burke to a superior moral status. From this base, Burke harnesses the power of history and judgment to prepare his entrance into the public realm.

The satiric tone in this second narrative is as strong as anywhere in the *Letter to a Noble Lord*. Since he has been so prompted, Burke welcomes the opportunity to turn our eyes to history "in which great men have always a pleasure in contemplating the historic origins of their house." Resting our gaze on Bedford's ancestry, we discover a house tainted from its inception by the avaricious spirit of Henry VIII. If the Hanoverian reign, to which Burke claimed allegiance, exemplified the principles of the Glorious Revolution, Henry VIII represented all that was counter to it. And it was from

Henry, Burke reminds us, that Bedford's House received its first reward. "The lion," Burke writes, "having sucked the blood of his prey, threw the offal carcass to the jackal in waiting. Having tasted once the food of confiscation, the favorites became fierce and ravenous." Bedford's original grant drew from a tyrant who plundered the church, confiscated private lands, and systematically exploited the goodwill of his subjects. However small, Burke's pension was made possible by a sovereign mild and benevolent. But more than a contrast in rulers, Burke's narrative makes clear the contrast in merit: "The merit of the origin of his Grace's fortune was in being a favorite and chief advisor to a prince who left no liberty to their native country." Conversely, Burke argues, he himself had worked to preserve not only "those rights in this chief seat of empire, but in every nation, in every land, in every climate, language, and religion, in the vast domain that is still under the protection, and the larger that was once under the protection, of the British crown." As the parallels widen, we note that Burke almost imperceptibly collapses the order with its representative; Bedford and Burke are synecdochically related to their respective histories. And insofar as Bedford's has been vanquished by the Glorious Revolution, his claim to the sanctions of the past are rendered obsolete. Burke, however, is centered within a new historical context, one that rewards merit, public virtue, and character.

The Argument Reconfigured

The course of Burke's argument has been directed by this effort at character construction and character destruction. By relegating the duke to a vanquished order, Burke in effect dislodges him from the position he occupied at the beginning of the *Letter*. Where once Bedford commanded the strength of his status, he becomes now a parasite to the order he represents; now odious, he may be indulged as pathetic. This kind of turnabout, of course, is familiar to apologia. Burke is quick to make the most of Bedford's weakness and against him casts the French contagion. But without close attention we are apt to miss the importance of this maneuver; Burke's attack is not against Bedford. The *Letter* has transformed its own rationale and has reconfigured the very terms of the contest. In brief, Bedford's weakness is England's weakness, and by honing in on Bedford, Burke acts to alert his countrymen to an insidious foe. In this way Burke avoids personal rancor, elevates the debate, and portrays himself to be acting just as he acted in the past. Personal defense at this point would be irrelevant; Burke is now in a position to act with positive force. Bedford's sympathy for the French revolutionists, Burke insists now, is more than inconsistent: it is dangerously ignorant and threatens the very order that protects him. Blind to history and human nature, Bedford, like England, remains oblivious and vulnerable. Burke does not despair of England's future should she awake and defend her venerable Constitution. However, Burke writes, "if the rude inroad of Gallic tumult, with its sophistical rights of man to falsify the account, and its word as a make-weight to throw into the scale, shall be introduced into our city by a misguided populace, set on by proud great men, themselves blinded and intoxicated by a frantic ambition, we shall all of us perish and be overwhelmed in a common ruin." And if, as Burke points to Bedford, "a great storm blow on our coast, it will cast the whales on the strand, as well as the periwinkles. His Grace will not survive the poor grantee he despises,—no not for a twelvemonth."

As Burke, Cassandra-like, warns of the French threat, Bedford becomes a pitiful and ironic victim. Burke in turn acts as the herald of England's safety, once again the statesman negotiating policy within the constraints of political community. The ironic twist is now a revolution, morally, politically, and rhetorically. Burke is no longer the victim of private insult; he is a champion of English liberties and tradition. His active role made necessary by French designs and English torpor, Burke returns to a public space he has helped to create. And the *Letter*, tumultuous and seemingly out of control, has served Burke's progress well. Within its economy, the dispute has been transformed into a battle for England's soul, and its players reconfigured into competing possibilities. Far from the "proud and insulting foe" mentioned earlier in the *Letter*, Bedford has become England's weakest moment, quarreling about pensions when its life is at stake. For this reason, Burke's question is ironic, a fact punctuated by the allusion to Pope's *Essay on Man* (I. 83–84); but more important, it situates his rationale for action in the political world: "Is it not a singular phenomenon," Burke asks, that

whilst the sans-culotte carcass-butchers and the philosophers of the shambles are pricking their dotted lines upon his hide, and, like the print of the poor ox that we see in the shop windows at Charing Cross, alive as he is, and thinking no harm in the world, he is divided into rumps, and sirloins, and briskets, and into all sorts of pieces for roasting, boiling, and stewing, that, all the while they are measuring him, his Grace is measuring me,—is invidiously comparing the bounty of the crown with the deserts of the defender of his order, and in the same moment fawning on those who have the knife half out of the sheath? Poor innocent! "Pleased to the last, he crops the flowery food, / And licks the hand just raised to shed his blood."

Thus Burke's *Letter* nears its conclusion at a very different level from where it began. What we may in other instances renounce as sheer invective we take here to be an ingenious transformation. Collapsing worlds both private and public, Burke thrusts the argument up and beyond the level of the particular. Personal apologia becomes defense of English constitutional monarchy; rancor is transformed into a rationale for political action.

Conclusion to the Letter

The recreation of Burke's character is now so complete that he can distance himself from terms of his own argument. Having achieved his vindication, Burke can redirect our attention away from issues of character specifically to principles of action. Never one to conduct his argument at the level of abstraction, however, Burke locates his principles in the form of another character—one Lord Keppel. In this way Burke is able to embody the principles for which he has contended and to do so without appearing, like Bedford, vainglorious. Now deceased, Keppel is resurrected by Burke as an exemplary figure, as much a counterpart to Bedford as he is a complement to Burke. Lord Keppel is a figure created in Burke's own likeness, meant to display those ideal virtues that alone can defeat revolutionary design. Like Burke, Keppel "valued the old nobility and the new, not as an excuse for inglorious sloth, but as an incitement to virtuous activity. He considered it as a sort of cure for selfishness and a narrow mind,—conceiving that a man born in an elevated place in himself was nothing, but everything in what went before and what was to come after him."

It is not until the final paragraphs that we learn that Lord Keppel was in fact Bedford's uncle. The disclosure provides a final ironic contrast, the last of many in the *Letter*. It also allows Burke to reassert himself into the *Letter* and to prepare for its closing lines. Now far from the original issue of the pension, Burke returns to Bedford. The stakes are very different now, and much greater. Whatever Bedford may now claim, Burke concludes, he "never shall, with the smallest color of reason, accuse me of being the author of a peace with Regicide. But that is high matter, and ought not to be mixed with anything of so little moment as what may belong to me, or even to the Duke of Bedford." And there is great irony.

Conclusion

This interpretation of Burke's *Letter to a Noble Lord* allows us to address three questions, in ascending degrees of generality. First, what can we now say of the author himself? The *Letter* grants access, however limited, to Burke's character, to his aspirations and failures, and indeed to his legacy. Not long after Burke had the *Letter* published, he wrote to a friend: "I give the matter to the disposition of the parties;—the style I abandon to the critics. I have done what I owed to my memory."[17] The intensely private tone evinced in those lines seems at times to overwhelm the public nature of the *Letter*, and we then catch sight of a bitter and haunted man. At the same time, we should recognize Burke as protecting his own character that he may protect his country's; and by attacking the character of Bedford, he had hoped only to alert England to a future imminent and strange.

Second, the *Letter* represents a significant example of the public letter as a rhetorical form. Most important, it illustrates the possibilities of the public letter to synthesize public and private impulses. In this sense, the rhetorical form incorporates knowledge gained from conditions of contemplation as well as appeals from the realm of action. One of the distinguishing characteristics of the public letter is that its generic boundaries are so flexible. Not surprisingly, the author can move from apologia to invective and back again, juxtapose theme and character, play private off public interests. The public letter reminds us that such generic conventions as apologia can be instantiated and combined in a variety of rhetorical forms without diminishing the persuasive force of those conventions.

In addition to what it can tell us about Burke the historical figure and about the public letter as a rhetorical form, the *Letter to a Noble Lord* invites a theoretical statement on the relationship between principle and action. We have found in the contours of its argument a unity of precept and appeal; and that unity, I have argued, is based upon the successful assertion of character into the interpretation of cultural change. The general significance of the *Letter*, therefore, is that it collapses so forcefully the public and the private, action and principle, rhetoric and philosophy. And it does so, not analytically, but in its very performance as an act of vindication and inducement. In this way, Burke's *Letter* fuses commitment to the general principles of British constitutional history with its specific argument for personal vindication.

In the end, Burke was seeking to reclaim for himself and his audience a lost world and its genteel virtues of individualism, civic action, and political responsibility. These virtues provide the commonplaces of the *Letter* and work to stabilize the wavering pieties of its readership. The principles that Burke invoked as an inducement to action may have been nostalgic; but like most forms of nostalgia, they were appealing in a time of great uncertainty, a moment of lament for virtues seemingly lost.

Epilogue
Burke's Discourse of Virtue

Virtue was for Burke an attribute of action. Best conceptualized as an adverb, it described the exercise of certain identifiable commitments. These commitments, in turn, provide for the "content" of virtue, defined as those actions that strengthened and ennobled the bonds of human community, that opened up and sustained the very possibility of public action. Conversely, those practices that threatened or damaged the conditions of community were to be regarded as virtue's opposite. The case studies this book examined help us to see not only how such a sense of virtue may be understood theoretically, but how it is deployed in and through the rhetorical arts. Virtue in this sense is indistinguishable from its expression in public discourse, because it is through the media of pamphlets, oratory, and public letters that the principle is activated and made meaningful. Thus virtue is a way of talking, a discourse of commitments that embraces the widest possible orbit of civic relations.

As a way of talking, as a discourse of commitments, in Burke's rhetoric virtue becomes a central term in the language of public life. It structures and constrains what gets talked about and to what end. As we proceed to engage in more detail this conception of virtue, it is important to keep in mind that while virtue has semantic content and propositional form, it is—if I have demonstrated anything in this study—fully realized only as it is activated rhetorically within the contexts of public argument.

As a kind of discourse, virtue at once constructs and is constructed. It provides a set of cultural commonplaces—what the ancient rhetoricians called topoi—that avail themselves to the description of a given act or actor. Virtue thus represents a range of symbolic resources, a deployable code used to describe attributes such as courage, prudence, and foresight. This vocabulary in turn situates and interprets public action. Virtue is itself historically and culturally situated; what counts as being virtuous in the eighteenth century is different from that in fifth-century Athens or twentieth-century America. But while its semantic content is variable, the appeal to virtue as a rhetorical resource remains a constant. This is so, at least in part, because virtue provides a way to make sense of political action. The discourse of virtue gives us a means to read and interpret the endless and often competing expressions of power. Its moral and persuasive force is a function of its descriptive possibilities; by naming a certain act virtuous, we identify the ground on which an action or individual is to be understood.

This process of designation, however, cannot be merely linear, as if virtue simply offered up a storehouse of ready-made and culturally given terms. Virtue is a construction, as subject to local pressures and aims as its object. It is a volatile and unstable code, modified or expanded according to its ends. By extension, the force of any given appeal to virtue will be contingent on the way in which virtue itself is understood. As a rhetorical construct, virtue must be positioned within an interpretive frame—it must be readable and strategic. At its most general level, this means that virtue gets contextualized, invoked through terms familiar to the immediate circumstances, and authorized by the exigencies they pose. More specifically, virtue gets constructed as it gets embodied and humanized, in effect, by being fixed within a recognizable form. Thus embodied, virtue at once finds its referent even as it takes on the shape and hue of that referent.

At the risk of oversimplifying the matter, I have chosen to stipulate as directly as possible the constitutive principles upon which Burke's discourse of virtue is based. Each principle is phrased as an expression of virtue in public life and is in turn examined according to the rhetorical form and function by which it is given force. The yield from such an approach allows us to identify the key terms of Burke's discourse, even as we see how those terms are symbolically managed. If, then, we were to construct a basic vocabulary of Burke's virtue, we need to isolate, on the basis of the six case studies offered here, the following terms.

That discourse is virtuous which sustains the conditions under which virtue is possible. This claim, to be sure, seems more formal than substantive as a description of Burke's discourse of virtue. But the very power of his *Thoughts on the Causes of the Present Discon-*

tents is to demonstrate that public action is in fact a good unto itself, that the capacity of a community to tolerate—ultimately to celebrate—a contest of opinions is an accomplishment of extraordinary proportions.

Burke's *Discontents* takes the reader a long way toward defining virtue as a quality of public life. It is in this sense a manifesto, not only of party government, but of the need to open up a public space of political action in which such organized beliefs might be articulated. When Burke looked at the structure of possibilities defining English politics in 1770, he saw that space threatened on at least two fronts. On the one hand he feared its eclipse by popular disorder and the attending loss of real leadership—hence his abiding distrust of Chatham. And on the other, more ominous front, he detected in Bute the systematic corruption of the polity by cabalistic intrigue and courtly consolidations of power. Both of these forces in effect forced the citizen out of politics and seduced him into one or the other extremities of power, the one too loud, the other too silent. Both failed to qualify as a legitimate basis for political action. Thus Burke sought in *Discontents,* as he did in numerous other works, to rationalize and give persuasive appeal to an optimal public space, a political condition without which virtue itself would not be possible.

The ostensible argument of the *Discontents*—that party politics is, far from being a necessary evil, in fact a positive good—bears out a more general set of implications for the discourse of virtue. As Burke contended for party against those who would usurp such expressions of organized power, he exemplified the virtue of that power. Put another way, *Discontents* both argues for, and in arguing for exemplifies, the virtue of public action. To the extent that the principle he promotes is expressed in the medium of public argument, he dramatizes its potential to help open and sustain the space of public action.

That action is virtuous which discloses public character. This somewhat abstract way of making my point can be made more useful by grounding it in Burke's 1774 *Speech on Taxation.* In it Burke teaches us that virtue is made meaningful and given rhetorical force as it is disclosed in public character. The portraits he paints with such artistry represent not virtue in the abstract—that indeed would run counter to Burke's way of apprehending reality—but virtue as it is literally embodied in its exemplars. We see in the aspects of Chatham, Grenville, North, et al., virtue's face, with all its variety and its opposites, its texture and its complexity. This countenance, this portraiture, reminds us that virtue in this specific sense is explicable only as it discloses and is disclosed. Burke reminds us too that virtue cannot be rendered independent of human agency, that it is an expression of character as character is made public.

The series of portraits that make up *Taxation* work to seize the narrative flow at key moments. Fixed at strategic places in his argument, the portraits allow the audience to pause and behold the guises of power. In this way Burke provides a way of reading virtue by repeatedly referring it to those who command it and give it expression—and to those who cannot. The portraits thus establish a means of reading virtue in the face of its exemplars. And as we gaze upon those faces, we see in striking detail the contours of power itself. Such a way of reading virtue casts the audience in a specific role, where it is positioned into an active spectatorship. In beholding the opposing portraits of Chatham and North, we are asked to make a choice and encouraged to make the right one. Burke's aim is aptly facilitated by his strategic use of the epideictic mode of address. The speech is, more than an extended review of taxation policy or an argument for imperial relations, a speech of praise and blame. The oration is accordingly multifaceted, a skillful interweaving of rhetorical forms as a way of rendering character into an expression of public virtue.

That action is virtuous which promotes standards of right reason. Burke's 1775 *Speech on Conciliation* stands as a hallmark of deliberative oratory, not least because it articulates a set of standards that oblige the audience to judge it in ways that exceed conventional measures of effect or success. The speech enacts the values it engages and asks the reader to assume an enlightened perspective that is consonant with the terms of the argument. Here then is a discourse of virtue that is at once pragmatic and visionary; it sets down standards for judgment and right reason even as it promotes a specific policy.

As an expression of virtue, rhetorical judgment is identifiable at both formal and functional levels. Its formal effect is to give coherence to principle in the face of change and dispersion. In this sense, the discourse of virtue holds forth a structure of commitments and makes those commitments appealing by the very image and display of that structure. This symbolic construction provides for a conspicuous rendering of judgment before others as a way of orienting and determining perspective. Burke's oration, then, may be understood as an especially clear instance of rhetorical judgment, by which I mean a subset stressing the performative and deliberative features of the broader category "political judgment." Because I propose Burke's speech as an exemplar of such judgment, it is worth elaborating briefly on this conception of judgment. The space between technical calculus and the bounded self is optimally the space of political judgment and the realm of the citizen, and its discourse is most appropriately deliberative. By extension, that discourse is virtuous which makes manifest its processes of reason, puts itself on display before those who are to judge it. Inevitably, in the process normative claims get promoted and standards of right reason get established as a way of assessing those claims. Burke's *Conciliation* tells us, finally, that deliberation, implicitly or explicitly, is always about what it means to deliberate, and when such discourse is thought wise, it may be said to qualify as an act of virtue.

That action is virtuous which sustains civic vision. For Burke, the capacity of community to envision its future and to act in such a way as to secure its prospects was basic to its success, and upon that capacity rested its claim to political virtue. By 1780 Burke had arrived at a fully developed sense of public time, and he gave that sense its fullest expression to date in his *Speech to the Electors of Bristol*. As always, he chose to articulate his ideas within the context of controversy and local concerns; the speech thus represents a particular response to a political exigence. As a result, the Bristol address is burdened with the weight of personal as well as public expectations. Apologiac in form and function, the speech is especially illuminating as an example of Burke's discourse of virtue, especially as a vindication of enlightened judgment in the service of civic vision.

Burke's choice to give expression to these principles in the midst of controversy over his own qualities of leadership may have been typical, but it gave distinctive force to his argument. Confronted as he was by a community grown suspicious of his leadership, Burke opted for a least likely scenario in which his ideas might gain acceptance. Burke's relationship to his audience, here and elsewhere, was seldom stable, and often in his career relationships proved, at least superficially, less than productive. From the time of his entrance into politics to his retirement in 1794, Burke seldom enjoyed much more than the indulgence of his listeners and readers; and if, as with his most successful efforts, he was able to command their respect, he was never able to secure it for long or without inciting the hostility of others less sympathetic. We might wonder, then, at the image of an embattled politician choosing to unfold a theory of representation before the very community calling him to account.

In order to make sense of Burke's speech at Bristol, we must understand his conception of the representative-represented relationship. That conception is expressed best by referring it to the rhetorical principle of audience. Contrary to those who would see the audience as either a passive receptacle of words or as determinative of the speaker's persuasive design, Burke understood the relationship between speaker and audience to be dynamic, unstable, and never taken for granted. But far from lamenting the uncertainty of this relationship, Burke acted upon it. If we can infer from his habitual modes of address, he believed the relationship to be most fully realized, most fruitful for both parties, when it existed in a state of tension. This was indeed its optimal moment, when both speaker and audience kept a sharp eye on each other and were vigilant in scrutinizing the claims being advanced and responsibilities assumed. Ultimately, such a relationship promoted a sense of mutual accountability, and here is where Burke entered most forcefully.

The *Speech to the Electors of Bristol* may be held up, as some have, as a flagrant example of political arrogance and disregard for the interests of the citizenry. While it is not my aim here to defend or sponsor the ideological implications of the speech, it is important to stress that such a claim drastically distorts, both historically and theoretically, its evident character. If we keep in mind Burke's conception of the optimal relationship between speaker and audience, it is quite clear that he saw himself involved in a classic confrontation of self-interest against community-interest. We need only attend to what was said in the speech to realize that its genius was to reconfigure the terms of that confrontation. Burke's aim was to restore the principle of community—here understood as polity in time—in the face of his audience's manifestly self-interested and short-sighted motives. The argument established the claim that the electors of Bristol had acted without regard to the long-term, without the vision necessary for political virtue. Conversely, his vindication was not a vindication of self only, but a defense of that conduct which located the interests of the community within the greater contexts of past and future. By confronting his audience, Burke exercised the necessary tension between himself, as representative, and his audience, as those whose concerns are being addressed. The result was to recall again the conditions under which accountability is made meaningful and necessary. The question may now be posed more usefully by asking how the speaker goes about such a reconstructive task.

The speech functioned rhetorically to reconstitute the symbolic space of virtue. This space, demonstrably opened in the course of the argument itself, was offered to the audience as a realm of possibilities, where enlightened judgment could be freely expressed and acted upon. It was accordingly a space where the representative, emancipated from the circumscribed and narrow limits of self-interest, could deliberate with a view. It thus afforded perspective and rewarded the community to the extent that it was willing to allow those who command it to act upon it. To the extent that this space was made available, the citizenry reclaimed for itself the ascription of virtue and saw in its chosen representative a mirror image of its own best self.

At its most potent, the discourse of virtue is celebratory. Even as every speech implicitly affirms the act of speaking, so virtue tends always to "speak itself." Virtue is in the most basic sense a symbolic principle, made meaningful when made public through the arts of effective expression. More than any other figure of his time, Burke grasped this relationship, and the rhetorical imperative that it entails. His prosecution of Warren Hastings makes dramatically clear that virtue loses nothing when it is, literally, staged. Burke accordingly conceived of virtue as an essentially rhetorical construct, most compelling when most visible. This staging was in the most positive sense aggressive; it required an act of assertion. Burke's attempt to wrap the Hastings impeachment in the resources of pageantry may thus be understood as fulfilling an obligation to the community of judges before him. By putting virtue on display, he celebrated it as a collective achievement. We are left to ask how such orchestration achieved its rhetorical ends.

To hold virtue before the community is to draw attention to relationships; more specifically, it is to announce what is the optimal order of things. By fixing Hastings within the gaze of the community and by juxtaposing his image against that of the speaker, Burke dramatized opposing values and gave them the face of human action and personality. In his own eyes, he was undertaking an act of restoration, an attempt to return collective values to their proper order. This reordering thus represents the positive counterpart to the work of disclosure and condemnation. Tearing off the veil of Hastings's venality, Burke was able to hold forth a more compelling image of that which had been hidden. He sought, in short, to make virtue observable again, open and accessible to all. In this sense, the rhetoric of the proceedings was to democratize the values it promoted.

Given the burden of his task, we cannot be surprised by the generic complexity that gave it shape. To the degree that Burke prosecuted evil and vindicated virtue, there was a clearly forensic force to his language. This quality, of course, was entirely consistent with the nature of the impeachment; we should not forget, however, that its forensic character was itself a feature of the drama. Burke literally gloried in his simultaneous roles as prosecutor and defender, and if there was an air of self-indulgence here, it was balanced by the affirmation of imperial law. Burke put justice on trial, and in effect he asked his audience to choose between those who would savage its dictates and those who would embrace its imperatives. There was a conspicuously deliberative resonance to the impeachment, and here

Burke was at home. As if to say that the future of the empire was at stake, Burke transformed Hastings's crimes from a matter of technical complaint into an issue for political judgment. The shift was essentially from time past to time future, where deeds done and now exposed can only be fully vindicated by securing against their recurrence. There was, then, in Burke's address a deliberative charge that his audience come together in an act of virtue and protect the commonweal from those who would threaten its integrity. Together, these forensic and deliberative functions provided a multifaceted base upon which the speaker was able to display, in true epideictic fashion, the essential virtues of his community.

The preceding descriptions of virtue stress Burke's commitment to public life and political action. I have chosen to emphasize as well the extent to which Burke understood these principles to be under pressure. At no point in his long career were these commitments allowed to become complacent; in fact, I would argue that Burke's discourse of virtue was most powerful precisely when he was being called to account. Virtue was for Burke public and unstable, and his pursuit of it inevitably drew him into the intersection of public action and individual will. The *Letter to a Noble Lord* stands as a compelling testimony to this pursuit and the struggle it required, for virtue as Burke understood it was an expression of individual will. If he knew that virtue presumed a public space in which it could be realized, he knew too that its origins lay deep in the spaces of private desire. Burke understood that acting virtuously meant acting with a knowledge of the stakes involved. As an expression of individual will, virtue was as contingent, momentary, and volatile as those who gave it voice.

In many ways Burke's *Letter* was a culmination. It compressed the synoptic descriptions of virtue rendered here into a furious declaration; it was an announcement of his own will to virtue delivered, not at the beginning, but at the conclusion of his life. It is perhaps too easy to read into that fact more pathos or tragedy than is evident in the text. But it does not stretch the point to acknowledge Burke's struggle to reinsert himself into the spaces of public life and to note the outrage that drove its rhetoric. The *Letter* vindicates not only individual will, but the commitments that give such will purpose and place. It is for that reason an exquisitely wrought representation of Burke's discourse of virtue, and it is ideally positioned here as an embodiment of the senses of virtue I have been discussing.

Six texts, six readings designed to illustrate Burke's discourse of virtue. Although so much more could be said, perhaps that is enough to restore Burke to his place, as I promised at the outset. Whether or not it is his rightful place, my aim in undertaking this book has been to position Burke where he inevitably positioned himself: in public. A political theorist of real stature, he gave voice to his principles where he was held personally accountable; an active politician, he chose as often as not to supersede or strain against the downward pull of political self-interest. Here, between theory and practice, Burke commanded his own unique place and commands it still. That is the space, too, of rhetoric, and in learning its ways, Burke learned how to give to virtue its most effective expression.

Notes

Introduction

1. For a review of Burke's reputation in modern scholarship, see Clara I. Gandy and Peter J. Stanlis, eds., *Edmund Burke: A Bibliography of Secondary Studies to 1982* (New York and London: Garland Publishing, 1983), 291–306.

2. See, for example, the aptly titled essay by Don Herzog, "Puzzling Through Burke," *Political Theory* 19 (1991): 336–63; the essay is one of several in a special issue devoted to Burke's political thought.

3. Important exceptions are: Steven Blakemore, *Burke and the Fall of Language: The French Revolution as Linguistic Event* (Hanover and London: University Press of New England, 1988); Christopher Reid, *Edmund Burke and the Practice of Political Writing* (New York: St. Martin's Press, 1985).

Chapter 1. Interpreting Political Culture in the *Present Discontents*

1. Edmund Burke, *Thoughts on the Causes of the Present Discontents*, in *The Works of Edmund Burke*, vol. 1 (Boston: Little, Brown, 1889). All citations sequential. As seems so often the case with Burke's discourse, his *Discontents* has commanded greater attention than its immediate reception, which was quiet, would suggest. Historians remain ambivalent about the precise status of the text as a public tract; Lecky pronounced it "one of the most valuable permanent contributions ever made to English political

philosophy," but confessed it to be "of very doubtful expediency" (W. E. H. Lecky, *A History of England in the Eighteenth Century*, vol. 3 [London: Longmans, Greene, 1902], 217–18); Harvey Mansfield embraces its rhetorical character, but only as a way of arriving at its historical truth: "The more rhetoric uncovered by inquiry into the literal meaning, the further such inquiry must proceed, for well-made rhetoric has an exact relation to the truth, and contains more, not less, than honest history" (Harvey Mansfield, *Statesmanship and Party Government: A Study of Burke and Bolingbroke* [Chicago: University of Chicago Press, 1965], 21); Donald C. Bryant, more sympathetic than most to Burke's practical aims, judged it to "stand among the four or five greatest politico-rhetorical pamphlets of a great age of political pamphlets" (Donald C. Bryant, "Burke's Present Discontents: The Rhetorical Genesis of a Party Testament," *Quarterly Journal of Speech* 42 [1956]: 116). Bryant's study is notable for detailing the composition of the text; it deals not at all with its modes of inducement, however, and is without interest as textual interpretation.

2. This approach relies in a general way upon the insights of James Boyd White, *When Words Lose Their Meaning: Constitutions and Reconstitutions of Language, Character, and Community* (Chicago: University of Chicago Press, 1984); in particular it affirms White's position that the "meaning of texts is thus not simply something found within it, to be dug out like a kind of mineral treasure, nor does it come from the reader, as if he were a kind of movie projector. It resides in the life of reading itself, to which both text and reader contribute" (p. 19). White's position is itself compatible with some, but not all, advances in reader-response theory and reception-aesthetics. See in this context Susan Suleiman, "Introduction: Varieties of Audience-Oriented Criticism," in *The Reader in the Text: Essays on Audience and Interpretation*, ed. Suleiman and Inge Crosman (Princeton: Princeton University Press, 1980); and Jane Tompkins, ed., *Reader-Response Criticism: From Formalism to Post-Structuralism* (Baltimore: Johns Hopkins University Press, 1980).

3. The most extensive treatment of virtue in these contexts is J. G. A. Pocock, *The Machievellian Moment: Florentine Political Thought and the Atlantic Republican Tradition* (Princeton: Princeton University Press, 1975); *Politics, Language, and Time: Essays on Political Thought and History* (New York: Atheneum, 1971); and *Virtue, Commerce, and History* (Cambridge, Mass.: Harvard University Press, 1985). See also Reed Browning, *Political and Constitutional Ideas of the Court Whigs* (Baton Rouge: Louisiana State University Press, 1983). Ian Shapiro, "Realism in the Study of the History of Ideas," *History of Political Thought* 3 (1982): 535–78, dissents from interpretations represented above.

4. White, *When Words Lose Their Meaning*, 19.

5. These interpretations are respectively represented by Frank O'Gorman, "Party and Burke: The Rockingham Whigs," *Government and Opposition* 3 (1968): 92–110; Richard Hofstadter, *The Idea of a Party System: The Rise of Legitimate Opposition in the United States, 1780–1840* (Berkeley and Los Angeles: University of California Press, 1969), 29; J. Steven Watson, *The Reign of George III, 1760–1815* (Oxford: Clarendon Press, 1960),

125; Herbert Butterfield, *George III and the Historians* (New York: Macmillan, 1959), 55; and John Brewer, "Party and the Double Cabinet: Two Facets of Burke's *Thoughts*," *Historical Journal* 14 (1971): 501. For a challenge to Brewer's conception of party, see J. C. D. Clark, "The Decline of Party, 1740–1760," *English Historical Review* 93 (1978): 499–527.

6. Flagrantly opportunistic readings of Burke for these purposes would include, on one end of the ideological spectrum, Russell Kirk, *The Conservative Mind, from Burke to Santayana* (Chicago: H. Regnery, 1953); and, on the other, Conor Cruise O'Brien, ed., *Edmund Burke, Reflections on the Revolution in France and on the Proceedings in Certain Societies in London Relative to That Event* (Baltimore: Penguin, 1969).

7. David Hume, "Of Parties in General," in *Essays, Moral, Political, Literary* (1741), quoted in J. A. W. Gunn, *Faction No More: Attitudes Toward Party in Government and Opposition in Eighteenth-Century England* (London: Frank Cass, 1972), 136.

8. Lord Halifax, "Maxims of State" (1700), quoted in Gunn, *Faction No More*, 43. In *Political Thoughts and Reflections* (1750), Halifax was even more direct: "The best party is but a kind of Conspiracy against the rest of the nation. . . . It turneth all Thought into talking instead of doing. Men get the habit of being unuseful to the Publick by turning in a Circle of Wrangling and Railing, which they cannot get out of" (quoted in ibid., 44).

9. See Alan Beattie, *English Party Politics* (London: Weidenfeld and Nicholson, 1970); Archibald Foord, *His Majesty's Opposition, 1714–1839* (Oxford: Clarendon Press, 1964); Caroline Robbins, "Discordant Parties: A Study of the Acceptance of Party by Englishmen," *Political Science Quarterly* 73 (1958): 505–29; and Gunn, *Faction No More*, for more detailed studies on the career of party politics in the eighteenth century.

10. Quoted in Beattie, *English Party Politics*, 20.

11. See John Brewer, "Rockingham, Burke, and Whig Political Argument," *Historical Journal* 18 (1975): 188–201; and Ross J. S. Hoffman, *The Marquis: A Study of Lord Rockingham, 1730–1782* (New York: Fordham University Press, 1973), 232–83 for an account of the Rockingham-Burke relationship.

12. This period of political and social instability is carefully portrayed by John Brewer, *Party Ideology and Popular Politics at the Accession of George III* (Cambridge: Cambridge University Press, 1976).

13. Letter of 29 October 1769 in Edmund Burke, *The Correspondence of Edmund Burke*, vol. 2, ed. Lucy Sutherland (Chicago: University of Chicago Press, 1969), 101.

14. On Chatham and Burke, see Butterfield, *George III*, 53–57; O'Gorman, "Party and Burke"; Watson, *The Reign of George III*, 125–26; Richard E. Willis, "Some Further Reflections on Burke's Discontents," *Studies in Burke and His Time* 11 (1969–70): 1417–27.

15. Brewer, "Party and the Double Cabinet"; Frank O'Gorman, "Edmund Burke and the Idea of Party," *Studies in Burke and His Time* 11 (1969–70): 1428–41.

16. On the character of conspiracy and its rhetorical force during the period, see Gordon Wood, "Conspiracy and the Paranoid Style in the Eighteenth Century," *William and Mary Quarterly*, 3d ser., 39 (1982): 401–41.

17. J. C. D. Clark, *The Dynamics of Change: The Crisis of the 1750's and English Party Systems* (Cambridge: Cambridge University Press, 1982), 4.

18. This constitution of ideal reader/audience is described in Edwin Black, "The Second Persona," *Quarterly Journal of Speech* 56 (1970): 109–19 and, more recently, in Peter Rabinowitz, *Before Reading: Narrative Conventions and the Politics of Interpretation* (Ithaca, N.Y.: Cornell University Press, 1987).

19. On the composition and relative power of eighteenth-century political publics, see P. D. G. Thomas, *The House of Commons in the Eighteenth Century* (Oxford: Clarendon Press, 1971).

20. Bernard Bailyn, *Ideological Origins of the American Revolution* (Cambridge, Mass.: Harvard University Press, 1967), 95.

21. For interpretive studies stressing Burke as the "philosopher-in-action," see Gerald Chapman, *Edmund Burke: The Practical Imagination* (Cambridge, Mass.: Harvard University Press, 1967); John MacCunn, *The Political Philosophy of Edmund Burke* (1913; reprint, New York: Russell and Russell, 1965); and Frank O'Gorman, *Edmund Burke: His Political Philosophy* (Bloomington: Indiana University Press; London: Allen and Unwin, 1973).

22. Burke's most famous attack on Chatham's administrative legacy was to come four years later in his "Speech on American Taxation" (in *Works*, vol. 2, 62).

23. A succinct analysis and useful review of this hermeneutic issue can be found in David Couzens Hoy, *The Critical Circle: Literature, History, and Philosophical Hermeneutics* (Berkeley and Los Angeles: University of California Press, 1978).

24. On the relationship between textual criticism and intellectual history, see Dominick LaCapra, "Rethinking Intellectual History and Reading Texts," *History and Theory* 19 (1980): 245–76; Roland Barthes, "From Work to Text," in *Textual Strategies*, ed. Josue Harari (Ithaca, N.Y.: Cornell University Press, 1979), 73–81, and, more recently with regard to rhetorical criticism, Dilip Parameshwar Gaonkar, "Object and Method in Rhetorical Criticism: From Wichelns to Leff and McGee," *Western Journal of Speech Communication* 54 (1990): 290–316.

Chapter 2. Reading Virtue and Rhetorical Portraiture in the *Speech on Taxation*

1. For background information see D. C. Bryant, *Rhetorical Dimensions in Criticism* (Baton Rouge: Louisiana State University Press, 1973), chap. 4; Burke, *Correspondence*, vol. 2, 530–31; Chauncey Goodrich, *Select British Eloquence* (Carbondale: Southern Illinois University Press, 1974), 214. For a treatment of the speech's publication, see Christopher Reid, *Edmund Burke and the Practice of Political Writing* (New York: St. Martin's Press, 1985), 118–20.

2. Horace Walpole, *Last Journals of Horace Walpole During the Reign of*

George III, From 1771–1783 (London: J. Lane, 1910), 1, 417–18; *Parliamentary History* 18, 215.

3. Goodrich, *British Eloquence*, 214; the *Monthly Review* 52 (1775): 83, wrote that the "speech altogether is a very able performance, and will fully answer all that may have been expected from the Author's abilities."

4. Dennis R. Bormann, "Portraits of Politicians: An Analysis of Three Character Sketches in Burke's Speech 'On American Taxation,'" *Dahlhousie Review* 56 (1976): 35, 45; Burke's portraiture is treated briefly in A. P. I. Samuels, *Early Life, Correspondence and Writings of Edmund Burke* (Cambridge: Cambridge University Press, 1923): 16.

5. Goodrich, *British Eloquence*, 214.

Chapter 3. Enacting Rhetorical Judgment in the *Speech on Conciliation*

1. Rockingham to Burke, 22 March 1775, Burke, *Correspondence*, vol. 3, 139.

2. James Ritcheson, *British Politics and the American Revolution* (Norman: University of Oklahoma Press, 1954), 190.

3. Watson, *The Reign of George III*, 201.

4. G. H. Guttridge, "The Whig Opposition in England During the Revolution," *Journal of Modern History* 6 (1934): 6.

5. For general studies of Burke and the circumstances surrounding the speech, see James T. Boulton, *The Language of Politics in the Age of Wilkes and Burke* (London: Routledge and Kegan Paul, 1963), esp. 1–7; John Brewer, *Party Ideology and Popular Politics at the Accession of George III* (Cambridge, Mass.: Cambridge University Press, 1976); Browning, *Political and Constitutional Ideas of the Court Whigs*; Bryant, *Rhetorical Dimensions in Criticism*, esp. 44–188; Hoffman, *The Marquis*, esp. 317–25; Frank O'Gorman, *The Emergence of the British Two-Party System, 1760–1832* (London: Arnold, 1982).

6. For studies of Burke as a "philosopher-in-action," see Chapman, *Edmund Burke: The Practical Imagination*; MacCunn, *The Political Philosophy of Edmund Burke*; Frank O'Gorman, *Edmund Burke: His Political Philosophy*; and Burleigh T. Wilkins, *The Problem of Burke's Political Philosophy* (Oxford: Clarendon Press, 1967); Carl Cone, *Burke and the Nature of Politics: Age of the American Revolution* (Lexington: University of Kentucky Press, 1957), 284–85.

7. Daniel V. Thompson, ed., *Burke's Speech on Conciliation with America* (New York: Henry Holt, 1923), 87.

8. Burke, "Speech on Moving Resolutions for Conciliation With America," in *The Works of Edmund Burke*, vol. 2 (Boston: Little, Brown, 1889), 101–102. All references to the speech come from this edition and hereafter are indicated parenthetically within the text.

Chapter 4. *Speech to the Electors of Bristol:* The Space of Rhetorical Virtue

1. For background studies on Burke and Bristol, see Sir Ernest Barker, "Burke and Bristol: A Study of the Relations Between Burke and His Constituency During the Years 1774–1780," *Essays in Government* (Oxford: Clarendon Press, 1951), 155–204; Hugh Owen, *Two Centuries of Ceramic Art in Bristol* (London: Bell and Daldy, 1873); Peter T. Underdown, *Bristol and Burke* (Bristol: Historical Association, 1961); and George E. Weare, *Edmund Burke's Connection with Bristol, from 1774 till 1800* (Bristol: William Bennett, 1894). All references to the text are from Burke, *Works*, vol. 2.

2. Studies of Burke and representation include Hannah Pitkin, *The Concept of Representation* (Berkeley and Los Angeles: University of California Press, 1967); Lucy Sutherland, "Edmund Burke and the Relations Between Members of Parliament and Their Constituencies," *Studies in Burke and His Time* 10 (1968): 1005–21.

3. Burke, *Correspondence*, vol. 4, 274.

4. *Monthly Review* 63 (1780): 385.

5. An illuminating analysis of Burke's address to the electors of Bristol may be found in Bryant, *Rhetorical Dimensions in Criticism*, chap. 5.

6. See Michael C. Leff and Andrew Sachs, "Word's the Most Like Things: Iconicity and the Rhetorical Text," *Western Journal of Speech Communication* 54 (1990): 252–73.

7. John Paul De Castro, *The Gordon Riots* (London: Oxford University Press, 1926).

8. *General Evening Post*, 8 June 1780, 2.

9. Reid, *Edmund Burke and the Practice of Political Writing*, 214.

10. Stephen H. Browne and Michael C. Leff, "Political Judgment and Rhetorical Argument: Edmund Burke's Paradigm," in *Argument and Social Practice: Proceedings of the Fourth SCA/AFA Conference on Argumentation*, ed. J. Robert Cox, Malcom O. Sillars, and Gregg B. Walker (Annandale, Va.: Speech Communication Association, 1985), 193–210.

Chapter 5. Staging Public Virtue in the Impeachment of Warren Hastings

1. *Macauley's Essay on Warren Hastings*, ed. William H. Hudson (New York: D. D. Heath, n.d.), 136.

2. Burke, *Correspondence*, vol. 5, 150.

3. Ibid., 151.

4. Ibid., 204.

5. See P. J. Marshall, *The Impeachment of Warren Hastings* (London: Oxford University Press, 1965), 112.

6. Accounts of the speech may be found in Mervyn A. Davies, *Strange Destiny: A Biography of Warren Hastings* (New York: G. P. Putman, 1935),

393–94; Sir Keith Grahme Feiling, *Warren Hastings* (London: Macmillan; New York: St. Martins, 1954), 343–60; Marshall, *Impeachment*, 64–87; Penderel Moon, *Warren Hastings and British India* (New York: Collier Books, 1962), 192–203.

7. *London Times*, 15 February 1788.

8. Ibid., 16 February 1788.

9. *European Magazine and London Review*, February 1788, 126.

10. All references to the text are from Burke, *Works*, vol. 9.

11. Fanny Burney, *Fanny Burney's Diary*, ed. John Wain (London: Folio Society, 1961), 176.

12. Davies, *Strange Destiny*, 393–94.

Chapter 6. Political Virtue as Rhetorical Action in the *Letter to a Noble Lord*

1. Donald C. Bryant, "The Contemporary Reception of Edmund Burke's Speaking," in *Historical Studies in Rhetoric and Rhetoricians*, ed. Raymond F. Howes (Ithaca, N.Y.: Cornell University Press, 1961), 282.

2. Lecky, *A History of England*, vol. 3 (London: Longmans, Greene, 1902), 417.

3. Francis P. Canavan, *The Political Reason of Edmund Burke* (Durham, N.C.: Duke University Press, 1960), 18.

4. Charles Parkin, *The Moral Basis of Burke's Political Thought* (New York: Russell and Russell, 1968), 3.

5. Donald C. Bryant, "Edmund Burke: New Evidence, Broader View," *Quarterly Journal of Speech* 38 (1952): 435–45.

6. C. I. Gandy, *Edmund Burke and the Whig Historians* (Ph.D. diss., University of Tennessee, 1973), Dissertation Abstracts International, 34, 08a.

7. O'Gorman, *Edmund Burke: His Political Philosophy*, 19.

8. Burke, 12 March 1796, *Correspondence*, vol. 8, 414.

9. James T. Boulton, "Edmund Burke's Letter to a Noble Lord: Apologia and Manifesto," *Burke Newsletter* 8 (1967): 695–701; Chapman, *Edmund Burke: The Practical Imagination*, 237–41; J. J. Fitzgerald, "Burke's Neglected Masterpiece," *Discourse* 8 (1965): 92–99.

10. John Morley, cited in Peter J. Stanlis, "Burke's Prose Style," *Burke Newsletter* 4 (1963): 181–84; B. Newman, *Edmund Burke* (1927, reprint, Freeport, N.Y.: Books for Libraries Press, 1969), 308; Ross J. S. Hoffman and Paul Levack, eds., *Burke's Politics* (New York: Alfred Knopf, 1949), 512; F. L. Lucas, *The Art of Living: Four Eighteenth-Century Minds* (New York: Macmillan, 1960), 192; MacCunn, *The Political Philosophy of Edmund Burke*, 4.

11. James T. Boulton, "The Letters of Edmund Burke: 'Manly Liberty of Speech,'" in *The Familiar Letter in the Eighteenth Century*, ed. H. Anderson, P. B. Daghlian, and Irwin Ehrenprise (Lawrence: University of Kansas Press, 1966), 186–209; Bryant, *Rhetorical Dimensions in Criticism*; Rob-

ert P. Fulkerson, "The Public Letter as a Rhetorical Form: Structure, Logic, and Style in King's Letter From Birmingham Jail," in *Rhetorical Dimensions in Media*, eds. Martin J. Medhurst and Thomas W. Benson (Dubuque, Iowa: Kendall Hunt, 1984), 296–313.

12. Cone, *Burke and the Nature of Politics*, 486–508; Thomas W. Copeland, *Our Eminent Friend Edmund Burke* (New Haven, Conn.: Yale University Press, 1949); Phillip Magnus, *Edmund Burke* (London: John Murray, 1939), 286–302.

13. Ian Christie, *Myth and Reality in Late Eighteenth-Century Politics* (Berkeley and Los Angeles: University of California Press, 1970); R. R. Dozier, *For King, Court, and Country: The English Loyalists and the French Revolution* (Lexington: University of Kentucky Press, 1983); C. Emsley, "Repression, 'Terror,' and the Rule of Law in England During the Decade of the French Revolution," *English Historical Review* 100 (1985): 801–24; Michael Freeman, *Edmund Burke and the Critique of Political Radicalism* (Oxford: Basil Blackwell; Chicago: University of Chicago Press, 1980).

14. Cone, *Burke and the Nature of Politics*, 445–53.

15. David McCracken, "Rhetorical Strategy in Burke's Reflections," *Yearbook of English Studies* 1 (1971): 120–24.

16. All references to the text are from Burke, *Works*, vol. 5.

17. Burke, *Correspondence*, vol. 8, 395.

Bibliography

Bailyn, B. *Ideological Origins of the American Revolution.* Cambridge, Mass.: Harvard University Press, 1967.

Barker, E. "Burke and Bristol: A Study of the Relations Between Burke and His Constituency During the Years 1774–1780." *Essays in Government,* 155–204. Oxford: Clarendon Press, 1951.

Barthes, R. "From Work to Text." In *Textual Strategies,* ed. J. Harari, 73–81. Ithaca, N.Y.: Cornell University Press, 1979.

Beattie, A. *English Party Politics.* London: Weidenfeld and Nicholson, 1970.

Black, E. "The Second Persona." *Quarterly Journal of Speech* 56 (1970): 109–19.

Blakemore, Steven. *Burke and the Fall of Language: The French Revolution as Linguistic Event.* Hanover and London: University Press of New England, 1988.

Bormann, D. R. "Portraits of Politicians: An Analysis of Three Character Sketches in Burke's Speech 'On American Taxation.'" *Dahlhousie Review* 56 (1976).

Boulton, J. T. "Edmund Burke's Letter to a Noble Lord: Apologia and Manifesto." *Burke Newsletter* 8 (1967): 695–701.

———. *The Language of Politics in the Age of Wilkes and Burke.* London: Routledge and Kegan Paul, 1963.

———. "The Letters of Edmund Burke: 'Manly Liberty of Speech.'" In *The Familiar Letter in the Eighteenth Century,* ed. H. Anderson, P. B. Daghlian, and I. Ehrenpreis, 186–209. Lawrence: University of Kansas Press, 1966.

Brewer, J. *Party Ideology and Popular Politics at the Accession of George III.* Cambridge, Mass.: Cambridge University Press, 1976.

———. "Party and the Double Cabinet: Two Facets of Burke's *Thoughts.*" *Historical Journal* 14 (1971): 479–501.

———. "Rockingham, Burke, and Whig Political Argument." *Historical Journal* 18 (1975): 188–201.

Browne, S. H., and M. C. Leff. "Political Judgment and Rhetorical Argument: Edmund Burke's Paradigm." In *Argument and Social Practice: Proceedings of the Fourth SCA/AFA Conference on Argumentation,* ed. J. R. Cox, M. O. Sillars, and G. B. Walker, 193–210. Annandale, Va.: Speech Communication Association, 1985.

Browning, R. *Political and Constitutional Ideas of the Court Whigs.* Baton Rouge: Louisiana State University Press, 1983.

Bryant, D. C. "Burke's Present Discontents: The Rhetorical Genesis of a Party Testament." *Quarterly Journal of Speech* 42 (1956): 115–26.

———. "The Contemporary Reception of Edmund Burke's Speaking." In *Historical Studies in Rhetoric and Rhetoricians,* ed. Raymond F. Howes, 271–93. Ithaca, N.Y.: Cornell University Press, 1961.

———. "Edmund Burke: New Evidence, Broader View." *Quarterly Journal of Speech* 38 (1952): 435–45.

———. *Rhetorical Dimensions in Criticism.* Baton Rouge: Louisiana State University Press, 1973.

Burke, Edmund. *The Correspondence of Edmund Burke.* ed. Thomas W. Copeland, Lucy Sutherland, et al. 10 vols. Cambridge: Cambridge University Press; Chicago: University of Chicago Press, 1958–78.

———. *The Works of Edmund Burke.* Boston: Little, Brown, 1889.

Burney, F. *Fanny Burney's Diary.* ed. John Wain. London: Folio Society, 1961.

Butterfield, Herbert. *George III and the Historians.* New York: Macmillan, 1959.

Canavan, F. P. *The Political Reason of Edmund Burke.* Durham, N. C.: Duke University Press, 1960.

Chapman, G. W. *Edmund Burke: The Practical Imagination.* Cambridge, Mass.: Harvard University Press, 1967.

Christie, I. *Myth and Reality in Late Eighteenth-Century Politics.* Berkeley and Los Angeles: University of California Press, 1970.

Clark, J. C. D. "The Decline of Party, 1740–1760." *English Historical Review* 93 (1978): 499–527.

———. *The Dynamics of Change: The Crisis of the 1750's and English Party Systems.* Cambridge: Cambridge University Press, 1982.

Cone, C. *Burke and the Nature of Politics: Age of the American Revolution.* Lexington: University of Kentucky Press, 1957.

———. *Burke and the Nature of Politics: The Age of the French Revolution.* Lexington: University of Kentucky Press, 1964.

Copeland, T. W. *Our Eminent Friend Edmund Burke.* New Haven, Conn.: Yale University Press, 1949.

Davies, M. A. *Strange Destiny: A Biography of Warren Hastings.* New York: G. P. Putman, 1939.

DeCastro, John Paul. *The Gordon Riots.* London: Oxford University Press, 1926.

Dozier, R. R. *For King, Court, and Country: The English Loyalists and the French Revolution.* Lexington: University of Kentucky Press, 1983.

Emsley, C. "Repression, 'Terror,' and the Rule of Law in England During the

Decade of the French Revolution." *English Historical Review* 100 (1985): 801–24.

Feiling, K. G. *Warren Hastings.* London: Macmillan; New York: St. Martin's Press, 1954.

Fitzgerald, J. J. "Burke's Neglected Masterpiece." *Discourse* 8 (1965): 92–99.

Foord, A. *His Majesty's Opposition, 1714–1839.* Oxford: Clarendon Press, 1964.

Freeman, M. *Edmund Burke and the Critique of Political Radicalism.* Oxford: Basil Blackwell; Chicago: University of Chicago Press, 1980.

Fulkerson, R. P. "The Public Letter as a Rhetorical Form: Structure, Logic, and Style in King's Letter from Birmingham Jail." In *Rhetorical Dimensions in Media,* ed. Martin J. Medhurst and Thomas W. Benson, 296–313. Dubuque, Iowa: Kendall Hunt, 1984.

Gandy, C. I. *Edmund Burke and Whig Historians.* Ph.D. diss., University of Tennessee. Dissertation Abstracts International, 1973.

Gandy, C. I., and P. J. Stanlis, eds. *Edmund Burke: A Bibliography of Secondary Studies to 1982.* New York and London: Garland Publishing, 1983.

Gaonkar, D. "Object and Method in Rhetorical Criticism: From Wichelns to Leff and McGee." *Western Journal of Speech Communication* 54 (1990): 290–316.

Goodrich, C. *Select British Eloquence.* Carbondale: Southern Illinois University Press, 1974.

Gunn, J. A. W. *Faction No More: Attitudes Toward Party in Government and Opposition in Eighteenth-Century England.* London: Frank Cass, 1972.

Guttridge, G. H. "The Whig Opposition in England During the Revolution." *Journal of Modern History* 6 (1934): 1–13.

Harari, J., ed. *Textual Strategies.* Ithaca, N.Y.: Cornell University Press, 1979.

Herzog, Don. "Puzzling Through Burke." *Political Theory* 19 (1991): 336–63.

Hoffman, Ross J. S. *The Marquis: A Study of Lord Rockingham, 1730–1782.* New York: Fordham University Press, 1973.

Hoffman, Ross J. S., and Paul Levach, eds. *Burke's Politics.* New York: Alfred Knopf, 1949.

Hofstadter, R. *The Idea of a Party System: The Rise of Legitimate Opposition in the United States, 1780–1840.* Berkeley and Los Angeles: University of California Press, 1969.

Hoy, D. C. *The Critical Circle: Literature, History, and Philosophical Hermeneutics.* Berkeley and Los Angeles: University of California Press, 1978.

Hudson, W. H., ed. *Macauley's Essay on Warren Hastings.* New York: D. D. Heath, n.d.

Kirk, R. *The Conservative Mind, From Burke to Santayana.* Chicago: H. Regnery, 1953.

LaCapra, D. "Rethinking Intellectual History and Reading Texts." *History and Theory* 19 (1980): 245–76.

Leff, M. C., and A. Sachs. "Words the Most Like Things: Iconicity and the

Rhetorical Text." *Western Journal of Speech Communication* 54 (1990): 252–73.

Lecky, W. E. H. *A History of England in the Eighteenth Century.* 8 vols. London: Longmans, Greene, 1902.

Lucas, F. L. *The Art of Living: Four Eighteenth-Century Minds.* New York: Macmillan, 1960.

McCracken, D. "Rhetorical Strategy in Burke's Reflections." *Yearbook of English Studies* 1 (1971): 120–24.

MacCunn, J. *The Political Philosophy of Edmund Burke.* 1913. Reprint. New York: Russell and Russell, 1965.

Magnus, Phillip. *Edmund Burke.* London: John Murray, 1939.

Mansfield, H. C. *Statesmanship and Party Government: A Study of Burke and Bolingbroke.* Chicago: University of Chicago Press, 1965.

Marshall, P. J. *The Impeachment of Warren Hastings.* Oxford: Oxford University Press, 1965.

Medhurst, M., and T. W. Benson, eds. *Rhetorical Dimensions of Media.* Dubuque, Iowa: Kendall Hunt, 1984.

Moon, P. *Warren Hastings and British India.* New York: Collier Books, 1962.

Namier, Sir Lewis. *The Structure of Politics at the Accession of George III.* London: Macmillan; New York: St. Martin's Press, 1957.

Newman, B. *Edmund Burke.* 1927. Reprint. Freeport, N.Y.: Books for Libraries Press, 1969.

O'Brien, C. C., ed. *Edmund Burke, Reflections on the Revolution in France and on the Proceedings in Certain Societies in London Relative to That Event.* Baltimore: Penguin, 1969.

O'Gorman, F. "Edmund Burke and the Idea of Party." *Studies in Burke and His Time* 11 (1969–70): 1428–41.

———. *Edmund Burke: His Political Philosophy.* Bloomington: Indiana University Press; London: Allen and Unwin, 1973.

———. *The Emergence of the Two-Party System, 1760–1832.* London: Arnold, 1982.

———. "Party and Burke: The Rockingham Whigs." *Government and Opposition* 3 (1968): 92–110.

Owen, Hugh. *Two Centuries of Ceramic Art in Bristol.* Bristol: Historical Association, 1961.

Parkin, C. *The Moral Basis of Burke's Political Thought.* New York: Russell and Russell, 1968.

Pitkin, H. *The Concept of Representation.* Berkeley and Los Angeles: University of California Press, 1967.

Pocock, J. G. A. *The Machievellian Moment: Florentine Political Thought and the Atlantic Republican Tradition.* Princeton, N.J.: Princeton University Press, 1975.

———. *Politics, Language, and Time: Essays on Political Thought and History.* New York: Atheneum, 1971.

———. *Virtue, Commerce, and History.* Cambridge, Mass.: Harvard University Press, 1985.

Rabinowitz, P. *Before Reading: Narrative Conventions and the Politics of Interpretation.* Ithaca, N.Y.: Cornell University Press, 1987.

Reid, C. *Edmund Burke and the Practice of Political Writing.* New York: St. Martin's Press, 1985.

Ritcheson, J. *British Politics and the American Revolution.* Norman: University of Oklahoma Press, 1954.

Robbins, C. "Discordant Parties: A Study of the Acceptance of Parties by Englishmen." *Political Science Quarterly* 73 (1958): 505–29.

Samuels, A. P. I. *Early Life, Correspondence, and Writings of Edmund Burke.* Cambridge: Cambridge University Press, 1923.

Shapiro, I. "Realism in the Study of the History of Ideas." *History of Political Thought* 3 (1982): 535–78.

Stanlis, P. J. "Burke's Prose Style." *Burke Newsletter* 4 (1963): 181–84.

Suleiman, S. "Introduction: Varieties of Audience-Oriented Criticism." In *The Reader in the Text: Essays on Audience and Interpretation*, ed. Susan Suleiman and Inge Crosman. Princeton, N.J.: Princeton University Press, 1980.

Sutherland, L. "Edmund Burke and the Relations Between Members of Parliament and Their Constituencies." *Studies in Burke and His Time* 10 (1968): 1005–21.

Thomas, P. D. G. *The House of Commons in the Eighteenth Century.* Oxford: Clarendon Press, 1971.

Thompson, D. V., ed. *Burke's Speech on Conciliation with America.* New York: Henry Holt, 1923.

Tompkins, J., ed. *Reader-Response Criticism: From Formalism to Post-Structuralism.* Baltimore: Johns Hopkins University Press, 1980.

Underdown, P. T. *Bristol and Burke.* Bristol: Historical Association, 1961.

Walpole, H. *Last Journals of Horace Walpole During the Reign of George III, From 1771–1783*, ed. A. Francis Stewart. London and New York: J. Lane, 1910.

Watson, J. S. *The Reign of George III, 1760–1815.* Oxford: Clarendon Press, 1960.

Weare, G. E. *Edmund Burke's Connection with Bristol, From 1774 till 1800.* Bristol: William Bennett, 1894.

White, J. B. *When Words Lose Their Meaning: Constitutions and Reconstitutions of Language, Character, and Community.* Chicago: University of Chicago Press, 1984.

Wilkins, B. T. *The Problem of Burke's Political Philosophy.* Oxford: Clarendon Press, 1967.

Willis, R. E. "Some Further Reflections on Burke's Discontents." *Studies in Burke and His Time* 11 (1969–70): 1417–27.

Wood, G. "Conspiracy and the Paranoid Style in the Eighteenth Century." *William and Mary Quarterly*, 3d ser., 39 (1982): 401–41.

———. *The Creation of the American Republic, 1776–1787.* New York: W. W. Norton, 1969.

Index

Abstraction: as a mode of reasoning, 47, 56–60, 102

Aesthetics: as a standard of judgment, 45, 46, 66

America: character of, 55–58; education in, 59; religion in, 59; tax policy toward, 28–66, 70, 76–77; spirit of, 59

Apologia, 69, 111–16, 121–22

Aristotle, 63, 65

Artistry: as a rhetorical trait, 2, 3, 5, 102, 107, 119. *See also* Aesthetics

Audience, 106, 121–22; appeals to multiple conceptions of, 147–48. *See also* Reader

Bailyn, Bernard, 19

Bathurst, Henry, 1st Baron Apsley, 2nd Earl Bathurst, 55–56

Beauchamp, Lord (Francis Seymour Conway), 70, 71, 77–78

Bedford, 5th Duke of (Francis Russell), 106–15

Bedford Party, 14

Bolingbroke, 1st Viscount (Henry St John), 13, 99

Bormann, Dennis, 29

Bristol, 9, 41, 67–82, 121–22

Bryant, Donald C., 128 (n. 1)

Burke, Edmund: and discourse of virtue, 5–10, 117–25; legacy, 1–3; in natural law tradition, 101–03; works: Impeachment of Warren Hastings, 9, 83–98, 123–24; *Letter to a Noble Lord,* 10, 99–116, 124; *Present Discontents,* 7–8, 11–26, 118–19; *Speech on Conciliation,* 3–4, 8, 45–66, 120–21; *Speech on Taxation,* 8, 27–44, 119–20; *Speech to the Electors of Bristol,* 9, 67–82, 121–23

Burney, Fanny, 97–98

Bute, 3rd Earl of (John Stuart), 15, 20

Cabal, 20, 21, 22, 23, 25, 119

Canavan, Francis, 101

Cataline, 10

Catholic Relief Act, 4, 71

Catholics, 72–81

Cavendish Bentinck, William Henry, 3rd Duke of Portland, 68, 73

Character, 8, 27, 37, 44, 52, 107–16, 120

Chatham, 1st Earl of (William Pitt, the Elder), 119–20; as victim of court intrigue, 20; Burke's attack on, 12, 15, 25; and Burke's portrait of, 38–41

Cicero, 10

Coleridge, Samuel Taylor, 2

Commonplaces, 6, 21, 24, 56, 104, 116–17

Milton, 60, 62, 65
Montesquieu, de, Baron de La Brede et, 99
Monthly Review, 68
More, Thomas, 62
Morely, John, 101, 104

Nabob of Arcot, 83
Namier, Sir Lewis, 2, 102
Narrative, 19–21, 28–30, 55–59, 75–81, 110–15
Natural Law, 101–03
Navigation Acts, 33
North, Frederick, styled Lord North, 8, 14, 32, 33, 47–50, 53, 119–20
Nostalgia, 65, 116

O'Gorman, Frank, 103
Oratory, 2, 4, 8, 28, 45, 117; and classical form, 49–50
Order, 86–87, 94, 108, 110
Ovid, 65

Paine, Thomas, 2
Parkin, Charles, 102
Parliament: ancient constitution of, 54; its failure to reason wisely, 42, 52; procedures of, 30, 90; policies of, 47; speech before, 9
Party, 7, 8, 11, 13; politics of, 11–26
Pathos, 34, 41, 108, 124
Patriotism, 24
Penal Codes, 71, 79–81, 101
Performance, 45, 48, 67, 74, 116
Perspective, 55, 80, 82; historical, 49–51, 56, 58
Petty, William, 2nd Earl of Shelbourne, 14
Philosopher-in-action, 25
Philosophy, 25, 81, 99, 100–03
Pitt, William, the Elder, 1st Earl of Chatham, 119–20; as victim of court intrigue, 20; Burke's attack on, 12, 15, 25; and Burke's portrait of, 38–41
Pitt, William, the Younger, 99, 107
Plato, 62
Pocock, J. G. A., 7
Pope, Alexander, 114
Portland, 3rd Duke of (William Henry Cavendish Bentinck), 68, 73
Portraiture, 8, 27–44, 119–20
Prudence, 12, 48, 68, 72

Reader, 11–13, 16, 21–26, 29, 34. *See also* Audience
Reformation, 7
Reid, Christopher, 81
Relationships, 8, 13, 16–17, 21, 23, 26. *See also* Reader
Representation, 9, 21, 63; Burke challenged on commitment to, 67–82
Revenue Act, 33, 42
Ritcheson, James, 46
Rockingham, 2nd Marquess of (Charles Wentworth Watson), 29, 36–39, 45, 84
Rockingham Whigs, 12, 14, 22, 48, 63–64; in opposition, 32; ministry, 14–15, 31, 61, 105; policy, 9, 31, 44, 52
Russell, Francis, 5th Duke of Bedford, 106–15

St John, Henry, 1st Viscount Bolingbroke, 13, 99
Satire, 112
Saville, Sir George, 71, 80
Shelbourne, 2nd Earl of (William Petty), 14
Space, 67–68, 84, 122–23, 125
Spectatorship, 34, 74
Stamp Act, 14; Grenville and, 34; passing of, 42; repeal of, 31–32, 36, 38, 42, 51–52
Stephens, Sir Leslie, 2, 101
Stuart, John, 3rd Earl of Bute, 15, 20
Sympathy, 19, 70, 94
Synechdoche, 51, 61, 87, 109

Theory, 3, 5, 6, 57, 58, 60, 63
Times, 85–86
Townshend, Charles, 8, 29, 31, 41–43

Virgil, 55–56, 65
Virtue: Burke's implicit theory of, 5–10; discourse of, 117–25

Walpole, Horace, 14, 28
Watson, Charles Wentworth, 2nd Marquess of Rockingham, 29, 36–39, 45, 84
White, James Boyd, 12, 128 (n. 2)
Wilkes, John, 14, 72

Xanthippe, 57

About the Series

STUDIES IN RHETORIC AND COMMUNICATION
General Editors:
E. Culpepper Clark, Raymie E. McKerrow, and David Zarefsky

The University of Alabama Press has established this series to pub-lish major new works in the general area of rhetoric and communi-cation, including books treating the symbolic manifestations of political discourse, argument as social knowledge, the impact of ma-chine technology on patterns of communication behavior, and other topics related to the nature or impact of symbolic communication. We actively solicit studies involving historical, critical, or theoreti-cal analyses of human discourse.

About the Author

Stephen H. Browne is Associate Professor of Speech Communication, Pennsylvania State University. He received a B.S. from the University of Oregon, M.A. from Colorado State University, and Ph.D. from the University of Wisconsin-Madison.